Drugs, children and families

Jane Mounteney and Harry Shapiro

VENTURE PRESS

Published by
VENTURE PRESS
16 Kent Street
Birmingham
B5 6RD

British Library Cataloguing-in-Publication Data
A catalogue record for this book is available from the
British Library

ISBN 1-86178-013-3 (paperback)

Design, layout and production by:
Hucksters Advertising & Publishing Consultants,
Riseden, Tidebrook,
Wadhurst, East Sussex TN5 6PA

Cover design by:
Western Arts, 194 Goswell Road
London, EC1V 7DT

Printed in Great Britain

Contents

Preface

This book is primarily geared towards child care social workers with the aim of increasing their knowledge and understanding and informing their practice around drug and alcohol issues. However, good practice in work with drugs, children and families requires a partnership approach with a range of agencies working together. The writers assume the reader to have a reasonable level of child care knowledge which they hope will be enhanced and supplemented by time spent considering the ways that both legal and illegal drugs may affect the lives of their clients. Specifically, *Drugs, Children and Families* aims to provide practical information on drugs and drug-using as this relates to the care given to the pregnant drug user; as this assists in the assessment of risk for a child in a drug-using environment; and finally as this helps to inform strategies for dealing with drug use among young people in a social work context.

The authors acknowledge that this practice guide raises far more questions than it answers. This seems inevitable in a relatively young and ever-changing area of social work practice, where there are no easy answers or magical solutions as to the best way of dealing with problem drug use. Social workers will be used to working with some degree of uncertainty or, put more positively, with a range of options, and tailoring their professional interventions and responses to individual needs and requirements. We hope this book helps those working directly with children and families to ask useful questions, make informed interventions, and know where to go to get further help and advice.

Acknowledgements

Sections of this book have been published as *Drugs, Pregnancy and Child Care* by ISDD in 1995 (revised edition). The authors would particularly like to thank Gerry Christian for her help in preparing this volume, also Alasdair Cant of Westminster Social Services Training Department, Sheila Durr and colleagues in the Bow/Poplar North assessment and family support team, Tower Hamlets SSD, and colleagues at ISDD.

Jane Mounteney and Harry Shapiro

The policy context

Social work practice with drugs, children and families is underpinned by a number of major pieces of legislation and policy.
While the Children Act (1989) and Working Together (1991) prescribe the child-centred focus and emphasis on joint and co-ordinated working between all agencies involved in child care work at a local level, the Community Care Act (1991) lays down the assessment and case management responsibilities for working with adult drug and alcohol users, including parents. The importance of a partnership approach is given new impetus from the drugs angle, via the government White Paper, Tackling Drugs Together (1995). Amongst other things, this three year drug strategy for England (Scotland and Wales have their equivalents – Meeting the Challenge 1994 and Forward Together 1996) has required the setting up of local multi-agency policy and implementation teams – Drug Action Teams (DATs) and Drug Reference Groups (DRGs) – to facilitate a co-ordinated approach to local drug use issues. DATs tend to be based on either health authority or local authority boundaries and the majority employ a co-ordinator. Membership of these teams, which have responsibilities in a number of areas pertinent to drugs, children and families, may include social services staff at all levels. The specific structure and remit of DATs and DRGs may vary a little from area to area: most will cover drug policy, planning, multi-agency training, service development. To contact your local DAT, try either the health authority or ask your director of social services(!), who will have been invited to attend.

Section One

The pregnant drug user

CASE STUDY ONE

Donna and Stephen are both white British and both have a history of drug and alcohol use involving a wide range of drugs. There is also a significant history of domestic violence where Stephen was stabbed by Donna, the injury required several stitches and an overnight stay in hospital. Donna tested positive for HIV six years ago, she probably contracted the virus as a result of sharing needles. The virus did not seem to affect her health for several years, but she now has AIDS symptomatic infection and has periods of feeling very unwell, although she can feel fine in between.

Donna and Stephen came to the attention of social services through a pre-birth conference, the outcome of which was registration under the category of likelihood of physical abuse and neglect.

At the review conference social services were informed that Monica was well and healthy. There were no complications, such as withdrawal symptoms at birth. The physical care of Monica was good and there were no concerns regarding her health.

Stephen detoxed from drugs (polydrug use) and both spent a period in a rehabilitation unit where they were able to take Monica. Both, however, continue to drink. They have a small family network. Stephen's grandfather sometimes looks after the baby although this is not always a satisfactory arrangement, mainly because he sometimes feels dumped on at short notice. There is a good professional network. Donna was less successful with the detox and her health continues to deteriorate. The relationship between Donna and Stephen also gives cause for concern.

SOME POINTS FOR CONSIDERATION

There are a number of complicating factors in this situation, and the need for a comprehensive assessment is paramount, as are regular network meetings as a number of agencies are involved and good communication is vital. This can be taken to the extent of a written agreement being drawn up with the parents about who will do what. The health visitor can continue to monitor Monica's progress. Some respite care for Monica could be offered to the family via a Family Centre or a sponsored child minder. If Donna and Stephen can cope with the involvement of different agencies, then they might be encouraged to attend or maintain contact with a suitable drug agency and an appropriate HIV agency, such as Body Positive, which may be able to offer specialist support to Donna.

The pregnant drug user and antenatal care

What do we mean by 'pregnant drug user'? Any woman who smokes cigarettes and drinks coffee during her pregnancy could be called a 'pregnant drug user'. In the context of this guide and involving those women who are most likely to be in need of social services, we mean women who are dependent on drugs, to the point where obtaining the money for drugs, buying and using them, and then experiencing the effects form a major part of their daily activity. These women may use heroin or a range of other drugs including alcohol and tranquillisers. In truth, most long term drug users are actually 'polydrug users', taking whatever drugs are available or that they can afford at the time.

Both drug users and non-users alike may experience ambivalent feelings about their pregnancy, especially if it is their first. While many women experience happiness and fulfilment, others experience great anxiety and fear surrounding their change of role, their ability to parent, and the changes a new baby may bring to existing relationships and children. Financial and housing difficulties can further add to these very real anxieties. For the woman who is dependent on drugs or alcohol, all these potential problems can be aggravated by her drug use, and where illegal drugs are concerned, the risky lifestyle that goes with it.

THE UNEXPECTED PREGNANCY

Women who use drugs, especially those using opiates, may have reduced fertility and irregular or absent periods. As a result they may not consider it necessary to use contraception under the illusion that they cannot get pregnant. It can be a shock, therefore, for some women drug users to find they are pregnant. For a proportion of these women, this can cause sufficient emotional turmoil as to make it unrealistic to expect immediate and lasting abstinence from sources of coping such as drugs or alcohol.

At this stage the woman may fear that the child or existing children may be taken from her should her drug use become known to health or social work staff. The woman might completely withdraw from caring agencies or be suspicious of the motives of those workers with whom she does come into contact. The situation won't be helped if the woman is assessed at social services offices, in the vicinity of the child protection team!

ENCOURAGING TAKE-UP OF ANTENATAL CARE

Many pregnant drug users do not attend for antenatal care, presenting instead in late pregnancy or even in labour. There are a number of possible reasons for this. It could be that the woman was a 'late booker' because she did not realise she was pregnant. It could be that she comes from a cultural background which makes it difficult for her to leave the house of her own free will. However, the 'fear factor' is crucial in keeping drug-using women away from antenatal care services. For a first pregnancy, the woman will not know what to expect or will be influenced by what she hears on the local 'grapevine'. For subsequent pregnancies, previous experience of medical and social work staff will either facilitate or inhibit her antenatal attendance.

It is helpful for workers to know which statutory and non-statutory agencies, if any, the woman is already in contact with, and if none, what might be available. A partnership role between agencies, where each agency is aware of the complementary skills of the other, can only improve care to pregnant drug and alcohol users. It is important for social work and medical staff working with pregnant drug users to adopt a caring and non-judgmental approach, with drug use being seen as a paediatric rather than a moral concern. Professionals' interventions relating to drugs and alcohol need to concentrate on what is likely to be the main concern of the woman – namely, the health of her baby. Pregnancy and childbirth may present a real chance for change for a parent – a window of opportunity which needs to be seized by workers.

PRINCIPLES OF ANTENATAL CARE

Care for pregnant drug users may be based in a drug agency or in a maternity unit. Whatever the local arrangements, the priority is to ensure good collaboration and communication between all agencies involved to maximise the effectiveness of the care offered. Often the biggest problem for a drug user is the organisational boundaries and the failure of agencies to offer accessible and seamless provision. As with any pregnant woman, antenatal care of the pregnant drug-user can be complicated by:

- lack of accurate dating of pregnancy
- late booking
- irregular attendance (or attendance at different hospitals, health centres, GPs or wherever antenatal care is provided, during the course of pregnancy)
- social problems
- homelessness and unemployment
- poor family experiences
- custodial care
- concealment of drug problems – applicable to the misuse of alcohol or tranquillisers as well as illegal drugs such as heroin or amphetamines.

Without avoiding possible health and social problems, workers need to ensure that pregnancy and birth are as normal and straightforward as possible for drug- and alcohol-using women.

Figure 1
Pregnant drug users and antenatal care – points to consider

- Are all pregnant women routinely asked about their use of legal and illegal drugs?
- In what ways (if any) should a pregnant user be treated any differently from any another woman presenting for antenatal care?
- Has the woman been informed about the risks to herself and the foetus of drug and alcohol use during pregnancy?

continued...

...continued

- What is the initial impression of the service for women drug users? Have they ever been asked?
- Is the woman clear what the different agencies expect of her? Has this been discussed with her without the use of jargon?
- Are the different agencies involved clear on their joint and individual roles or is more than one person trying to do the same job? Is one person responsible for co-ordinating care? Are all the relevant agencies involved? Are they in contact with one another, sharing skills and information? Does the woman know whom to ask for what?
- Is the woman aware of other helping agencies (non-medical and non-drug specific) – Citizens Advice Bureau's, law centres, nurseries, mother and toddlers groups, etc?
- If the woman is in poor housing, is she in contact with the local housing department or housing associations etc?
- If the woman is not working, is she getting the right benefits?
- If she is working, is she aware of her maternity rights? Does she wish to return to work, does she need help securing child care?
- If the woman appears to be on her own, is there a partner, friend or family who can offer support during the pregnancy and after?
- The whole thrust at present is to get HIV testing routinely offered in all antenatal clinics. Is it clearly signposted or explained that this is going on? Is there an option to refuse? Is the woman user treated differently for the test than other women, for example, are gloves used universally or only brought out to test the pregnant user?
- What happens to the woman who wishes to carry on using drugs? Will she be treated unsympathetically and be told her baby will be born addicted? It is important that the woman is informed about the risk of the baby going into withdrawal, what this entails and what her involvement will/can be. Will she be informed of less risky forms of drug taking and/or given access to treatment?
- All workers make judgements based on attitudes and experience. These attitudes need exploring.
- Workers need supportive supervision to deal with potential moral issues and dilemmas.

PROPOSED PROCEDURE GUIDELINES FOR WORK WITH PREGNANT WOMEN WITH PROBLEM DRUG USE

These were drafted by the Clinic Social Workers Group and are currently being revised (SCODA, 1997). The emphasis here is on collaborative case management.

---

1. BOOKING MEETING – WHEN PREGNANCY IS CONFIRMED

Membership (may include)

Drug agency worker; paediatrician; obstetrician; health visitor; community midwife; probation officer; social worker; GP; client and partner (or significant other).

Purpose

To identify pre-birth keyworker

To share information

To make an assessment of previous and current drug use

To discuss drug treatment options

To decide upon the need for a child protection case conference to be held before birth.

2. PLANNING MEETING – TWO MONTHS BEFORE EXPECTED DATE OF DELIVERY

Membership

As above, plus area social worker who will take over the case after discharge.

Purpose

To share the keyworker's assessment

To discuss short and long term plans

To decide upon the need for a child protection case conference to be held before discharge.

3. PRE-DISCHARGE MEETING – SOON AFTER THE BIRTH

Membership

As above plus paediatrician and special care baby worker.

Purpose

To assess bonding and the current situation

To ensure that appropriate care will be provided in the community

To confirm who will be the new keyworker

To decide whether a review meeting or a further child protection case conference is necessary.

4. REVIEW MEETING – THREE MONTHS AFTER

Membership

As above.

Purpose

Formal feedback and liaison.

These guidelines suggest that social services departments may find it useful to hold a planning meeting for information exchange once the pregnancy is confirmed, and also two months before the expected date of childbirth. Note, however, that child protection conferences will not be required for all drug-using women who become pregnant. A pre-birth child protection conference should be considered in circumstances where professionals have concerns about the future welfare of the unborn child. The mother and partner need to be told about all meetings and given the option to attend.

Departments will find that a written antenatal care policy for pregnant drug users has advantages for both social worker and drug user. The social worker will know what is expected and (so long as it is properly explained) the woman will know exactly where she stands in relation to the courses of action open to the worker in different circumstances.

Medical complications

Any pregnant woman living in poor circumstances (bad housing, unemployment, etc) can present with a range of medical problems and go on to give birth to a baby that is premature or 'small-for-dates'. These problems can be exacerbated by the effects of drugs and the chaotic lifestyle led by some (but not all) drug users.

FOR THE FOETUS (EFFECTS OF DRUGS)

It is difficult to establish clear and reliable information about the effects of drugs (including alcohol and tobacco) on the foetus, what quantities or what combinations are likely to cause damage, and safe levels of use. There are a number of reasons for this:

1. There are many problems with 'foetal damage' studies, including retrospective and self-reporting drug assessments, extrapolation from animal studies and the taking of inadequate histories of those women in the study.
2. Clinicians and public health officials often 'play safe' by simply stating what foetal damage has been reported after use of a particular drug without estimating how frequently it happens, often quoting rarely reported reactions or anecdotes of single cases. They fear that any attempt to discuss levels or frequencies of use will not only be seen as condoning use but will also be taken to imply that all will be well below some set limit – a guarantee that nobody can give.
3. There is also a moral dimension to what purports to be objective scientific evidence. An article in *The Lancet* (Koran et al, 1989) discussed research into the effects of illicit cocaine use on reproduction. It showed that research reporting adverse effects from use of the drug was more likely to be published in the scientific press than research that reported an absence of adverse effects, irrespective of the scientific validity of the research.

> *The general answer to a question like 'I took some x before I found out I was pregnant. Is it likely to hurt the baby?' is almost certainly no. But everything would depend on the drug, the amount taken over what period, and the individual physiology of the baby. One unfortunate aspect of over-emphasising the likelihood of adverse effects of drugs on the foetus is that it may persuade some concerned women to actively consider termination when they need not.*

Given these limitations, what follows is a review of the current state of knowledge about the possible effects of different drugs on the foetus.

GENERAL PROBLEMS WITH DRUGS

For pregnant drug users in general, irrespective of the drug used, and especially where poor social conditions prevail, there is an increased risk of:

- low birth-weight – low birth-weight can arise from prematurity and intra-uterine growth retardation ('small-for-dates'). Both are associated with potentially serious complications, such as increased susceptibility to infections and feeding problems
- perinatal mortality – death within the first week of birth. Prematurity is a significant contributor to perinatal mortality
- congenital abnormalities, which for drug users are in the 'high normal' range of 2.7 – 3.2% of all pregnant drug users who give birth. The main risk period for the development of such abnormalities is in the first three months of pregnancy when the foetus is actually forming and often even before the woman knows she is pregnant. After the first three months, when development of organs is complete, growth retardation may be a problem for the babies of pregnant users
- sudden infant death syndrome, also known as 'cot death' or SIDS.

DIFFERENT DRUGS

TOBACCO

There is no evidence that the risk of congenital abnormalities is increased by smoking cigarettes, although heavy smoking has been associated with:

- low birth-weight (babies less than 12.1 kgs). Those who stop smoking in the last three months of pregnancy are more likely to have babies at non-smoking weight averages than those who continue. Even so, most babies of even heavy smokers in pregnancy grow normally
- premature births (before 37 weeks)
- reduced oxygen supply to the foetus due to reduced levels of oxygen in the mother's blood. One study showed that even if smoking is stopped for only 48 hours, there is an 8% rise in available oxygen for the baby
- reduced blood flow because, as a stimulant, nicotine constricts the blood vessels
- perinatal mortality, mainly associated with low birth-weight, but some associations with tobacco have been claimed such as premature rupture of the placenta.

ALCOHOL

At all points along the continuum from occasional light drinking to regular heavy drinking, there is conflicting evidence as to the possibility of alcohol damaging the foetus. From the clinical studies undertaken, there would appear to be a large body of evidence to suggest an association between drinking and foetal harm; however, to quote the Department of Health Sensible Drinking report: A major problem in interpreting the human studies is the large number of confounding factors, including poor nutrition, licit and illicit drug intake and smoking, all of which have known adverse effects on pregnancy. (DH, 1995, p17.)

A serious compounding methodological problem is how one defines heavy drinking. Definitions vary from fewer than two units per day (Barrison et al, 1995) to 18 units a day (Rosett et al, 1978). In spite of the broad range of variables and sometimes conflicting evidence, the 1995 Sensible Drinking report makes a number of conclusions, including the following:

- There is general agreement that alcohol has the potential to induce the following effects: abortion; foetal growth retardation; facial and other dysmorphologies; and impaired post-natal physical and mental development.

- Most studies agree that two units per day and above may be associated with reduced birthweight. However, there is no good evidence that one or two units per week has any adverse effect.
- Studies suggest that binge drinking can also produce the effects listed above.

The recommendation is that women who are pregnant or likely to become pregnant should keep their alcohol intake substantially below limits suggested for non-pregnant women.

FOETAL ALCOHOL SYNDROME (FAS)

This expression was coined to describe a set of features that may present in a minority of babies whose mothers had been drinking heavily during pregnancy. According to the Royal College of Obstetricians and Gynaecologists (RCOG) guideline (1996) a FAS diagnosis requires signs in all of the four following categories:

- foetal growth retardation
- central nervous system involvement (neurological abnormalities, developmental delay, intellectual impairment, etc)
- characteristic facial deformity
- congenital abnormalities, principally heart deficiencies.

By no means all female heavy drinkers give birth to babies with full FAS. In the 10-year period to 1980, out of 50,000 deliveries at Hammersmith and Queen Charlotte's Maternity Hospitals in London, not one was a FAS baby (Bolton, 1987). This may be because FAS is under-recognised in Britain or because American clinicians are more ready to label a baby as demonstrating it. A less serious syndrome is known as FAE (Foetal Alcohol Effect). Even this is not inevitable among the babies of women who drink heavily. As regards interventions for pregnant alcohol-users, the RCOG recommends:

In pregnancy heavy alcohol consumers will require specific counselling and possible referral for specialist treatment. This is especially true for binge drinkers where the effects on the foetus remain uncertain, but will nonetheless cause concern to both mother and obstetrician. (RCOG, 1996, p3).

AMPHETAMINES

There appears to be a limited association between amphetamine use in pregnancy and congenital malformations – isolated cases of cleft palate and heart deficiencies. But there are no indications in the literature as to what dose and level of amphetamine use are most likely to lead to problems for the foetus.

BENZODIAZEPINE TRANQUILLISERS (VALIUM, LIBRIUM ETC)

Studies have shown a link between benzodiazepine use in the first period of pregnancy and a mouth deformation known as cleft palate. Chlordiazepoxide may be the safest of the tranquillisers in this respect, but all of them should be treated as having the potential to cause malformations. Breast-feeding can be a problem with cleft palate babies, but the condition is operable when the baby weighs 10 pounds or is three months old.

CAFFEINE

There is some limited evidence to suggest an association between caffeine consumption in excess of 300 mg a day (approx. five cups of instant coffee or tea or six cans of cola drinks) and a small decrease in birth weight. Irregular foetal heart rate has been associated with very large daily amounts of caffeine intake late in pregnancy, but this returns to normal when caffeine drinking has stopped.

CANNABIS

One of the more extensive studies into the effects of cannabis on the foetus was conducted in Canada over four years involving 700 women not from chronically deprived environments (Fried, 1986). When compared with a matched control group, there were no significant differences in rates of miscarriage, type of presentation at birth, frequency of obstetric complications, birth weight or physical birth defects even among the heaviest users (defined as those smoking six or more joints a week during pregnancy). There was some evidence of slightly shorter gestation period (about a week) among the heavy smoking group. The few studies which have suggested a range of adverse outcomes (prematurity, low birth weight etc) for the babies of heavy cannabis smokers have involved women whose drug taking, diet and general lifestyle have been more potentially detrimental to pregnancy outcome than those taking part in the Canadian study. As far as infant behavioural responses were concerned, it was noted in the Canadian study that the babies of the heaviest users were more easily startled than those of occasional or non-users, but were none the less easily comforted.

COCAINE AND CRACK

Possibly more than any other drug, heavy cocaine or crack use in pregnancy has been associated with harmful effects on the foetus. These may include premature rupture of the membranes, babies being delivered early, small-for-dates and under weight. Also, as cocaine is a powerful stimulant, restrictions in foetal growth have been observed which may be due to reduction in oxygen supply to the foetus caused by the blood vessels constricting. However, most of the research suggesting such associations has been conducted with women from very poor socio-economic backgrounds where the more general problems for their babies are also more likely to occur. Also many of the women in these studies had little or no antenatal care. There can also be problems for the babies of cocaine-using mothers in the postnatal period. They may feed poorly and be particularly difficult to comfort until they have been able to clear the drug from their system. There is conflicting evidence about developmental problems for those children born to cocaine- or crack-using mothers. Even 'worst case' studies from the USA are unable to prove conclusively that where problems occur they can be attributed to maternal cocaine use (Hutchings, 1993).

A study of social cocaine users (ie not dependent) who stopped when they realised they were pregnant, concluded that the social users *did not experience adverse pregnancy outcome above the rate expected in the general population'* (Graham et al, 1989, p143).

ECSTASY [MDMA]

There are no published case reports implicating use of Ecstasy in foetal damage.

HEROIN AND OTHER OPIATES

The only direct effect of opiate use in pregnancy appears to be low birth-weight babies. Other effects (prematurity etc) are more probably the result of additional factors such as poor diet and ill health. There is some evidence of growth retardation with heroin (Thornton et al, 1990). The effects on the foetus of maternal detoxification or withdrawal during pregnancy are explored in detail in Chapter 3. The notion of addicted babies is discussed in Chapter 4.

LSD

In the 1960s LSD was the subject of much press scaremongering. There is no evidence of foetal damage caused by LSD.

SOLVENTS

Inhaled solvents reduce oxygen levels in body tissue and easily cross the placenta, so sniffing during pregnancy theoretically might reduce oxygen supply to the foetal brain, although there appear to be no cases on record. However, there is a study by Goodwin (1988) which demonstrates an association between chronic daily paint-sniffing (toluene) for several months with renal problems in the newborn baby.

Effect of maternal withdrawal from drugs during pregnancy

HEROIN AND OTHER OPIATES

Actually withdrawing the woman from opiates during pregnancy is considered by some clinicians to be too dangerous for the foetus to cope with – even more dangerous than for the woman to carry on using. However, many women do want to come off drugs when they find they are pregnant – the pregnancy itself may be seen as an opportunity for a change of lifestyle. And the perceived dangers of withdrawal are not matched by experience of Glasgow's reproductive health service for women.

> *The first 300 drug-using women who delivered in the service included 164 women who underwent opiate detoxification in hospital one or more times at gestations from 5 to 39 weeks, 64 of whom underwent 'cold turkey' detoxification. Rates of foetal death, pre-term delivery and low birth weight were lowest in the 'cold turkey' detox group, higher in the methadone detox group and highest among women who did not undergo detoxification.*
>
> *These groups were self-selected and the impact of other variables is unquantifiable, so the results do not indicate that detoxification is safer than maintenance. However, the excellent outcomes in the detox group do indicate that antenatal detoxification is not unduly hazardous to the foetus and can be undertaken at any speed and at any time'*
>
> **(Hepburn, 1996 p13)**

WITHDRAWAL REGIME: INPATIENT V OUTPATIENT

As far as opiates are concerned, the consensus is that a slow in-patient withdrawal should be considered in the view of the risk of premature labour, foetal distress and death associated with abrupt withdrawal of opiates.

Heroin has a short action, which can mean repeated periods of withdrawal with potentially damaging effects on the foetus. Withdrawing from infrequent large doses of heroin presents a special risk of poisoning or overdose to the non-tolerant foetus.

Inpatient detoxification may be undertaken slowly (from four weeks onwards), although a mother-to-be may be advised to remain an inpatient for longer. The advantages of inpatient care are:

- the methadone dosage can be adjusted to prevent either intoxification or withdrawal symptoms
- the foetus can be monitored
- detoxification is more likely to be successful with less chance of additional illicit drugs being used on top of the prescription
- in-patient care can be particularly suitable for those whose social situation is unstable, although there is always the question of what happens when the woman returns to this unstable environment.

For those users who have good support at home, outpatient detoxification would be preferable. Such support could be provided by parents or relatives who will often 'rally round' in such circumstances. Support may come from a partner who is also withdrawing from drugs.

However, during the withdrawal period, particularly if detoxification is on an outpatient basis, the woman might be under a number of pressures, for example:

- her partner may still be using heavily. If her partner wishes to co-operate in helping the woman to withdraw, maintenance prescribing to the partner may be worth considering. It is likely that they will want half of the prescription the woman is given unless they are also receiving a prescription
- drug-using friends (who may be the woman's only ones) may give misguided support by supplying drugs to ease stress or anxiety, or by advising abrupt cessation. Any woman who wishes to detoxify herself should be advised against stopping all drugs suddenly. A suitable withdrawal regime could be worked out in collaboration with a drugs worker
- the woman needs to be warned that some of the physical symptoms of late pregnancy – backache, muscle pains, restlessness etc – can feel like withdrawal.

TREATMENT REGIME

Some high-dose and/or long-term opiate users may be best treated with methadone maintenance as otherwise the risk of returning to illicit drug use is high. These risks have to be balanced against that of the baby suffering opiate withdrawal if the mother is maintained on a stable dose of methadone throughout her pregnancy, or of a more severe or extended withdrawal syndrome if the woman merely adds methadone to continuing illicit use.

Inpatient and outpatient opiate detoxification is best conducted during the second three months of pregnancy as this minimises the risk of abortion and premature labour, although in practice it is not always possible to do this. Methadone is the drug usually prescribed; the drug acts over a longer period and so the risk of withdrawals between doses is reduced. It may be possible for prescriptions to be dispensed by a local chemist.

The outpatient user is likely to prefer a single daily dose rather than a split dose of methadone involving an additional visit. Reduction should again be slow with dosages being reduced at a rate no greater than 5 mg methadone per week. Again, complete detoxification would normally be expected within a period of 12 weeks.

Partial detoxification followed by maintenance on a low fixed dose of methadone, say 15 mg daily, has limited effects on the foetus and may be an ideal compromise solution. Some women who present too late for full detoxification may also fit into this category. The evidence shows that at doses of 15 mg or less, the baby is very unlikely to suffer withdrawal reactions.

BENZODIAZEPINES

When benzodiazepines have been taken in ordinary therapeutic doses, they should be withdrawn on an outpatient basis – this is usually achievable over a four week period. However, when they are taken in large amounts (eg 60 mg diazepam or more per day) inpatient withdrawal to prevent fits in the mother is appropriate.

STIMULANTS

Substitute withdrawal or maintenance is not appropriate for stimulant drugs (amphetamine or cocaine) and is potentially harmful to the foetus.

Postnatal care

The signs and symptoms of neonatal drug withdrawal are predominantly unspecific in nature and do not indicate a particular drug of dependence. It is unlikely that workers will be able to predict the extent of the withdrawal symptoms the baby of a drug using mother is likely to experience. However, the marked emergence of any of the following should prompt consideration of a neonatal withdrawal syndrome: sleeplessness, restlessness/irritability, sneezing, sweating, abnormally rapid heart rate, tremors, vomiting, yawning, fever, fist-sucking, hyperflexia, diarrhoea, nasal stuffiness, respiratory depression, and convulsions.

Of course, any of these features could be symptoms of something else – but they may be the first indication to the staff that the mother has been using drugs.

A baby is likely to develop an abstinence/withdrawal syndrome if the mother has been regularly taking cocaine, opiates, tranquillisers, barbiturates (or other sedative type drugs) during the later stages of her pregnancy. There is some evidence to suggest that even intermittent use by the mother can result in physical dependence in the foetus in that drugs seem to be concentrated by the foetus which has a less efficient metabolism. For this same reason, the emergence of the drug withdrawal syndrome in a newborn child may be delayed for many days if long-acting drugs (or long-acting active by-products) are still present in the infant's system.

It is important not to lose sight of the goal in the care of such a baby. The reluctance to prescribe any drugs (especially opiates) to the baby for fear of causing dependence is understandable, although this may be an emotional rather than a medical response. However, it must be remembered that the foetus will have been exposed to such drugs *in utero*. The baby will therefore need help when these drugs leave its system. The goal is to bring about a controlled withdrawal from the drug over a reasonably short period of time without causing unnecessary suffering or jeopardising the well-being of the infant.

The initial relationship between any mother and baby may be difficult for all sorts of reasons. At the postnatal stage, positive reassurance from staff is needed to support the development of bonding between her and her child. Contact between mother and child needs to be encouraged, including visits to the special baby unit, as bonding could be impeded if the baby is away from the mother being treated for drug withdrawal. The infant could appear distressed and irritable, and be more difficult to comfort than other babies in the ward because of the drug still her/his system The mother must be reassured that it is not her mothering which is at fault, but rather the physical state of her baby. Professionals will need to maintain a balanced and non-judgmental approach when working with these clients and avoid blaming the mother and indicating disapproval.

Where it exists, extended family support can be of great benefit – however, care needs to be taken to protect the confidentiality of the family. Drug users often fear telling their parents about their drug use – but their parents often know already what is going on and in any case will become most suspicious about, for example, a nine pound baby staying in a postnatal ward for several weeks. By no means are all babies born to drug-using women premature or 'small-for-dates'.

Section Two

Drugs and the family

CASE STUDY TWO

Sandra is a 24-year-old mother of two girls aged three and four. She has been using heroin for six years on and off. She was on a methadone reduction prescription just before her second child was born, but this was unsuccessful. The father of the first child has been in prison since she was born and the second father, Billy, belongs to Sandra's drug using circle of friends. Sandra has just completed a probation order in relation to cheque book fraud.

A neighbour contacts social services because she thinks the children have been left on their own. Sandra vehemently denies this, saying the neighbour bears a grudge against her after a dispute earlier in the year. She is deeply suspicious of social services, and can be antagonistic – even aggressive – towards outside professionals. Sandra does, however, admit that she has been having difficulties in coping recently and that whenever Billy is around her drug use goes up. She is starting to inject tranquillisers when she is not able to get the heroin she needs. The girls seem to be thriving, but Sandra is becoming increasingly reliant on a stepsister who looks after them from time to time.

SOME POINTS FOR CONSIDERATION

Sandra's drug use seems to be very bound up with Billy, which is not an uncommon scenario. Sandra's introduction to social services has been unpleasant, in the way that it has been notified, so the initial impressions will be important to her. It is crucial that Sandra gets a sense that having the interests of the children as being paramount does not necessarily work against her.

What is her interpretation of events? An assessment will have to be made which looks at the actual risk that might be posed to the two children, including how the drugs are stored, whether the children are left alone while drugs are being bought, etc. It cannot be assumed that the aggression towards authority figures is not also shown to children.

What other agencies are involved with Sandra? It is likely that she has had a good experience with Probation, and this might be a good place to start in terms of linking in with other agencies. Similarly, Sandra might well already be in touch with a drugs agency. The fact that she is having difficulty obtaining her heroin suggests that this might be a good opportunity to consider another methadone programme, which would give her a chance to stabilise her drug use and lifestyle. Previous failure on methadone is not unusual, and does not rule this out as an option. The support that the stepsister can give could be explored further and worked out in a more constructive way.

Issues on discharge from hospital

BREAST-FEEDING

Most drugs of misuse do not pass into the breast milk in quantities which are sufficient to have a major effect on the newborn baby. With opiates, for example, the quantities ingested are so small that they will not prevent the onset of the neonatal opiate withdrawal syndrome. Breast-feeding is encouraged in mothers who are using drugs as long as the use is stable and the breast-feeding is not suddenly stopped. There is some variation amongst the benzodiazepines. Diazepam passes into the milk and may cause sedation in the newborn. Chlordiazepoxide and nitrazepam also go into the breast milk, but in such small quantities that the baby remains unaffected.

Although, in general, it is much preferable for babies to be breast-fed (not least because it helps build up immunity to infection), women who are HIV positive or whose HIV status is unknown need to be informed of the risks of infecting the baby and are advised against breast-feeding. Studies show that if an HIV positive mother breast-feeds her baby, there is twice the risk of passing on the infection, especially if the mother has only recently been infected.

HIV/AIDS

Various studies show the risk of mother-to-baby transmission of HIV ranges from 14 to 39%. All infants born to HIV positive mothers will have maternal HIV antibodies; however, this does not necessarily mean they are infected.

'Historically, the diagnosis of HIV infection in babies has demanded follow-up for a minimum of 18 months to allow for the disappearance of passively transferred maternal antibodies. Those who are HIV positive after this time are infected with HIV'

(Carey, 1995)

There is a need for confidentiality in testing babies and infants because the mother is also being tested indirectly. For example, a child may be placed with foster carers and some time later test positive for HIV. In a worst-case scenario, the natural mother might come to hear about both her own and her child's HIV status second-hand, without the support of pre- or post-test counselling. For the purposes of social work assessment, it is important to note that HIV positive children tend to bruise easily, so care must be taken in assuming that physical abuse has occurred.

HEPATITIS

Hepatitis B is common among injecting drug users. The transmission routes are the same as for HIV, but the disease is even more infectious. Hepatitis B may be transmitted from mother to child, although prompt immunisation of babies of known carriers at birth has proved effective. If the baby is going to become infected with Hepatitis B (rather than just having maternal antibodies) this will happen during the first three months of life.

Hepatitis C is also common among injecting drug users and far more dangerous than Hepatitis B. Up to 50% of all carriers develop serious liver disease (Carey, 1995). Immunisation for Hepatitis C is not possible and the only reliable test to see if a baby is infected with Hepatitis C is a non-standard (and therefore expensive) PCR test.

SINGLE PARENTS

Single parents may be isolated from support systems and also may be so afraid of being identified as drug users that they will not approach nurseries or other forms of child care to give them some breathing space from children or perhaps time away from older children to care for a baby. A woman on her own may be stigmatised both as a drug user and a single parent.

UNEMPLOYMENT

Lack of a regular income for any family is likely to put that family under enormous pressure. If income is being supplemented by illegal activities such as shoplifting, or by prostitution, then these may bring with them additional difficulties. Women should be advised on their maternity and child benefit rights.

HOUSING

Workers looking after the social needs of drug-using families may well have to advocate for their clients in defence of their need for decent housing. Some drug users may lead relatively nomadic lives, moving from one insecure residence to another. In many cases, the best prognosis for stability is 'own front door', however, it would be unrealistic to imagine that simply moving a family to a 'drug free' estate is the answer to all its ills.

Workers should ensure that people who are HIV positive or who have AIDS are supported in their efforts to obtain secure and suitable accommodation. This is especially important for those living in insecure environments such as squats, whose need will be to keep stress levels down. It is important to utilise all possible sources of assistance, ie housing associations, local authority housing departments and the private sector as well as any specialist housing services. The possibility of medical priority as outlined in the 1977 Housing Homeless Persons Act should be looked into for people with HIV-related illnesses. Whether or not an HIV positive person is regarded as 'vulnerable' under the terms of the Act, will vary between local housing authorities. It may be difficult to secure priority for somebody who is HIV positive unless they are also demonstrably unwell.

Social work assessment of children in a drug-using environment

Drug use by parents does not automatically indicate child neglect or abuse. A social worker has to establish in what ways, if any, drug use is putting children at risk and what the role of drug use is in the life of the family.

There are a number of important concepts to have in mind when working with children in a drug-using environment. The first two are enshrined in the Children Act 1989:

- **significant harm** – a term used whereby the 'harm' suffered should be sufficient to warrant public intervention. It means ill treatment or impairment of health or development. Ill treatment also includes sexual abuse. Development is defined as physical, emotional, intellectual, social or behavioural, and health as mental or physical. The significance of the harm is to be measured and compared with that which could be reasonably expected of a similar 'hypothetical' child
- **child in need** – a person under the age of 18 is in need if they are unlikely to achieve or maintain, or have the opportunity of achieving or maintaining, a reasonable standard of health or development without the provision for them of services by a local authority or their health or development is likely to be significantly impaired or further impaired without provision of such services, or they are disabled.

A third concept more commonly used in the drugs and alcohol field:

- **harm minimisation** – an approach to working with drug users which is aimed at reducing the drug-related risks to their health. To stop using drugs is not always an acceptable or realistic option and therefore it is vital to find ways to reduce the potential harm associated with drug use. This may mean providing support, information and advice about issues broader than drugs – for example, to provide benefits and housing advice.

Automatic registration of the children of drug-using parents will deter these parents from approaching drug dependence clinics or other professionals for help. The grapevine is very important in communicating news about services among users. If a parent who uses drugs has sympathetic, non-judgemental treatment then this information will be passed along. Bad news, however, travels faster and so it is also important that all services have a clear policy in place for working with drug-using parents. Equally crucial is that parents. should know exactly what the position is. For example, if an agency has guidelines then these should be explained and given to the drug user so that they fully understand what the statutory obligations of a social worker are in the case of concern about a child. Some clients will be completely unaware of reasons for concern and this only serves to mystify and alienate a social work department from the client. In families where problem drug use is an issue, a comprehensive assessment of the relationship between parental drug use and child care is indicated. Where possible, the assessment is best carried out jointly by child care and adult workers.

CONFIDENTIALITY

The issue of confidentiality is a pertinent one for drug agencies, whose successful working with clients often depends on the maintenance of a confidential service. Adult users may be unwilling to attend an agency if they believe that their parenting skills will be scrutinised and social services informed. Most workers in drug and alcohol agencies or drug dependency clinics will not have any specialist child care training and may not be too clear on the extent of their statutory responsibilities.

If there are any concerns about the welfare of a child, statutory agency workers must inform social services and refer the case to them for assessment. In reality, no agency can guarantee complete confidentiality. There are circumstances when information must be disclosed, including occasions where there is concern that a child or other person is at risk or when the courts instruct disclosure (sometimes via the police).

ASSESSMENT

It is important to assess families where drug use is a problem in the same way as other families where possible child care concerns arise. On its own, problem drug or alcohol use is not an indicator of abuse or neglect. A social worker has to focus on the needs of the child and establish in what ways, if any, drug use is putting the child at risk, what the role of drug use is in the life of the family, and how this impacts on the parenting skills and child care. Inevitably, some drug-using parents will themselves be under 18 and so 'children' under the Act. Once the needs of the child have been identified, professionals can find ways to meet these and to support the parents and family members. If the evidence suggests the child is at risk, the agreed local child protection procedures need to be followed.

The assessment may take place over a period of time, allowing the worker to establish a relationship with the parent(s). The gathering of certain information requires workers to visit the client at home. If unannounced visits are anticipated, this needs to be made clear in initial contracts and agreements with the family.

SOCIAL WORK ASSESSMENT GUIDELINES FOR WORKING WITH DRUG-USING PARENTS
(ADAPTED FROM GUIDELINES DEVELOPED BY A GROUP OF SOCIAL WORKERS ATTACHED TO DRUG CLINICS – SEE **NLAFD, 1989.**)

Below, some of the most important points to consider when assessing families with drug use problem issues are laid out. The answers to individual questions must be put in the context of the whole family situation and decisions should not necessarily be taken on the strength of 'bad marks' in one area of the assessment. Drug users come from a range of ethnic and cultural backgrounds and assessments will need to be sensitive and tailored to make them appropriate to the client's needs. Finally, it is worth pointing out that the following assessment can be used as a means to educate parents and help avoid crisis situations arising.

1. THE PATTERN OF PARENTAL DRUG USE

● **is the drug use relatively 'stable' or 'chaotic' (ie, swings between states of severe intoxication and periods of withdrawal and/or polydrug use, including alcohol)?**
● **are the levels of child care different when the parent is using drugs and when not?**
● **is there a drug free parent or supportive partner?**

This first step is an attempt to separate drug use itself from problematic drug use. There are at least three identifiable patterns of drug use.

---

1. Some parents have a regular and stable pattern.
2. Other parents will take any type of drug in any amount depending on availability, resulting in very erratic behaviour.
3. The third type is where a life crisis precipitates problem drug use.

If we can distinguish between these three types, it is possible to identify specific areas of concern. This won't necessarily focus on what type of drug, or how much of it, is being used by parents, but rather it should enable workers to put drug use back into context, building up a broad picture of how much money is being spent, where it comes from, who gets the money, where the drugs come from, and where the child fits in.

Even though some parents may binge or misuse drugs and/or alcohol over an extended period, the direct effect on the child may be minimised where the parent has made arrangements for a partner or relative to take responsibility for child care. Conversely, where some established form of alternative child care is not in place, children whose parents may use fewer drugs less chaotically may, however, be more affected than the children of regular users. The wider context of child care can furnish very important clues about a family system.

CASE STUDY

A London social services department was in contact with the mother of a five-year-old child who was legally maintained on opiates, but periodically 'blitzed' the West End of London. She would become chaotic and the child had to be voluntarily accommodated by the local authority. *continued...*

> *continued...*
>
> In consultation with her worker, who was extremely well versed in
>   the type of drugs used, the cost, how she administered them,
>   and how she obtained the money, it was realised that she always
>   notified the social services before she started using illicit drugs in
>   a chaotic manner.
> It became clear, once drugs were put to one side, that at times of
>   emotional distress this woman felt unable to look after her child
>   and used her drug taking as a method of obtaining short-term
>   assistance from social services.

This case demonstrates the need for workers to look at the
reasons why, for instance, a generally stable user should
suddenly go on a drug binge. By viewing the drug use in
this case as a symptom rather than a cause, the focus of the
child care changed from a response to chaotic drug use to
looking at areas of pressure on the mother, such as grieving,
bereavement, and a need for planned short-term support.

Then again, it is not automatically the case that parents
are more capable without their drugs. Drug withdrawal
can have a severe effect on the capacity of parents to
tolerate stress and anxiety, and many parents certainly
believe this to be the case. Parents under the influence of
alcohol, however, may be more dangerous than when
sober, although there is no 'hierarchy of harm' and each
family should be dealt with on an individual basis.

Some parents who use amphetamines have said they
feel livelier and therefore more playful and in tune with
their children when using them, although parents'
perceptions may well be distorted.

2. ACCOMMODATION AND HOME ENVIRONMENT

● **is current accommodation adequate for children?**

Accommodation where residents have to be out of the house all
  day (for example, bed and breakfast) can hardly be considered
  adequate for either children or parents. Continued drug use
  under such circumstances would not be unexpected.

● **are parents ensuring that rent and bills are paid?**

If the answer is no, this could be for reasons other than the
  purchase of drugs.

● **does the family remain in one locality or move
frequently, and why?**

● **is the family living in a drug-using environment?**

There are some drug-using environments where high levels of
    drug dealing, violence, and criminality may place children at
    unacceptable levels of risk.

● **are other drug users sharing the accommodation?**

● **are the parents allowing their premises to be used by
other drug users?**

● **are the premises being used for selling drugs,
prostitution, etc?**

Concerns here include the proximity of children to
potentially harmful drug-related activity, for example drug
dealing in the home and strangers coming into the home.

However, health visitors have reported households
where drug taking was an acceptable fact of life. What
mattered here was that the parents had organised safe
child-care arrangements and that drug dealing and other
drug-related activities did not occur in the presence of the
children. Also, the presence of strangers was discouraged.

3. PROVISION OF BASIC NECESSITIES

● **is there adequate food, clothing and warmth for the
children?**

It has been observed by workers that drug-using parents can be
    extremely careful to attend to the physical needs of their
    children precisely because they feel they have to be more than
    perfect in order to demonstrate to social workers their
    adequacy as parents.

● **are the children attending school regularly?**

● **are the children engaged in age-appropriate activities?**

This could relate to both what the child is expected to do for the
    parent and whether or not drug use by the parents actually
    affects child development.

● **are the children's emotional needs being adequately met?**

The emotional needs of a child including basic love and affection
    may be compromised by a number of factors which put
    families under stress, including poverty, alcoholism and
    mental illness.

● **are the children assuming parental responsibility?**

Concerns here might include – does the child's daily life revolve
    round the parents' drug use, or are the parents ensuring the
    child's needs come first? To what extent is the child assuming
    inappropriate responsibilities?

The needs of children of drug-using parents are no different from those of any other child, although the drug issues can sometimes mask the needs. For example, the fact that a 12-year-old boy is collecting his mother's methadone maintenance prescription from the chemist may not necessarily indicate that the mother is physically incapable of collecting it herself. She may be at home looking after younger children. However, a child being sent to a drug clinic on the mother's behalf would be an example where inappropriate responsibility was being placed on the child.

In all child care cases, emotional needs are much harder to identify. Children who live in a home where there is considerable drug dealing may be able to relate on a superficial level to any adult, but may be unable to form deeper relationships with anyone.

Most children have fantasies and conversations with real or imaginary friends. They may also develop mature and productive relationships with adults. However, very young children in a drug-using environment may have such limited contact with their peers that the development of very sophisticated and continuous fantasy worlds can cause problems. Such a child's experience may have been of adults who are transient and often sick from withdrawing or 'high' whilst using drugs.

Care of siblings is another issue – **how old is the child doing the caring? How long are they in charge?** A responsible 14-year-old with lots of baby sitting experience may be very suitable for the job of looking after other children in the family. However, this should not be a task repeatedly given to the child to the extent that they are prevented from mixing with peers.

4. **HOW THE DRUGS ARE PROCURED**
   ● **are the children being left alone while the parents are procuring drugs?**
   ● **are the children being taken to places where they can be deemed to be at risk?**
   ● **how much are the drugs costing, and how is the money obtained?**

5. HEALTH RISKS

- where are the drugs normally kept?
- are the parents injecting drugs?
- are the syringes shared, and how are they disposed of?
- are the parents aware of the health risks associated with using drugs?

When considering health risks to children it is important to get away from the narrow approach of 'if they leave their drugs around the child may use them'. It is not just drugs themselves which present health risks. With HIV and hepatitis in the drug-using population, a range of health issues must be seriously considered. Parents should be made aware of the existence of specialist agencies, such as needle exchanges and disposal schemes which provide services, help and advice on drug-related health care matters.

6. FAMILY'S SOCIAL NETWORK AND SUPPORT SYSTEM

- do parents and children associate primarily with other drug users, with non-users, or with both?
- are relatives aware of the drug use and are they supportive?
- will the parents accept help from the relatives and other statutory/non-statutory agencies involved?

Further support systems should also be investigated – nurseries, day centres, social networks comprising other people with children. The stereotype of drug users not having families is false. Not only do they have children of their own, but they are often in touch with their wider family network. Consequently it is important not to overlook the positive aspects of this when considering what child care interventions are necessary.

7. WHEN IS INTERVENTION NECESSARY?

- are there grounds under one's own local authority's care procedures?
- are these appropriate for assessment?

8. THE PARENTS' PERCEPTION OF THE SITUATION

- do the parents see their drug use as harmful to themselves or their children?

- do the parents place their own needs before those of their children?
- are the parents aware of the local authority's child care procedures?

You can't play the game if you don't know the rules. What chances have the family been given to make changes in their life, before the children are accommodated by the local authority? Would residential rehabilitation be appropriate? Is there any chance of a house exchange to get away from the usual environment?

Many parents are afraid to seek help because of their uncertainty about the statutory response. Similarly, many social workers are unclear as to the full range of their duties and options in terms of working with this client group. All parties are likely to benefit from local authorities drawing up and disseminating a clear policy and procedures for the assessment of families where drugs or alcohol use is a problem. This policy should also be made known to clients and other professionals.

Social workers already have the skills for assessing child care cases, but many feel deskilled when faced with drug issues. This is exacerbated by a lack of training and clear agency policy and procedures, which can result in workers either ignoring drug use issues or over-reacting to them. In a similar vein, drug workers may feel deskilled when faced with child care issues. Historically, non-statutory drug services have been adult-focussed and have considered passing on information as a breach of confidentiality. As such they have often worked against, not with, social services. They have not always passed on information about risk to a child for fear of 'grassing up' clients. Then again, they may have witnessed social workers taking children into care unnecessarily, and so do not trust social services.

The partnership approach can prove the most useful tool here as regards pooling different professionals' expertise and ensuring good communication and building trust between all agencies involved in a case. Clear guidelines on passing on information and clear confidentiality statements are vital.

Following an assessment, social workers will be responsible for developing a care package which both meets the need of the child and supports the parents. When working with a parent who is seeking treatment for their drug problem, a social worker will need to investigate what local resources are available. Does the local drug clinic have any day care facilities? Is there any local child care provision or a local relative who could look after the children while the parent is in treatment. Even among estranged families, it can be at times like this, when the drug user is taking positive steps to stop using drugs, that families can come together again. Other options may include placement at a family centre to support parenting and allow for monitoring of the family or foster/respite care to provide a break on a planned or as needed basis.

Drug rehabilitation and families

Since 1993, as a result of the NHS and Community Care Act (1990), social service departments have been given the responsibility for undertaking assessments of need for people misusing drugs and alcohol in their local community, and tasked with devising individual care plans. They also have fundholding responsibilities as regards residential rehabilitation placements and a continued care management role with these clients.

FUNDING RESPONSIBILITIES

A 1996 survey by SCODA found that in a substantial number of local authorities, residential placements for drug users with children were not being funded. A range of problems and complexities relating to funding are cited, including:

- the lack of an identified budget for placing children while the parent is undergoing residential treatment
- lack of agreement to fund children by care managers, because such funding would take the total costs of the placement well above the notional cost limits
- reluctance to fund children from child care budgets because such placements do not fit criteria.

In the words of one children and families social worker:

> *'Responsibility for funding is a complete nightmare. Drug users want to come off immediately, but how fast can you get funding organised? If an adult drug user wants rehabilitation, the adult team do the assessment. If a child is involved, the children and families team have to do a separate assessment. This can take so long and be so fragmented. Then there is the problem as to whether services are available.'*

FAMILY BREAKUP

Unnecessary family breakups may occur when parents are referred for residential treatment or rehabilitation. This can involve them having to hand over the care of their children, temporarily, to a close relative or to the local authority because there are few facilities which enable a parent to detoxify while retaining direct responsibility for their children. In such circumstances it is important that regular contact is maintained between parents and the children during treatment.

If both parents are undergoing detoxification at the same time, they also have to cope with adjusting to a non-drug relationship, which is difficult enough without the responsibility of caring for children as well. The SCODA study found examples of clients relapsing as a result of the stress associated with inappropriate care arrangements for their children, or long delays getting arrangements agreed. Lack of support and provision for the children of drug users is an area that commissioners need to address.

If you are thinking of trying to refer a family to a residential rehabilitation house, then here are some issues to consider.

The child

1. What does the child want to do?
2. Is it better for the child to be in close contact with mother and/or father in the house, or sent to a close relative, or accommodated by the local authority?
3. If the child is accommodated on a voluntary basis and the mother leaves the rehabilitation house early because she doesn't get on there, will the mother be able to get her child back easily?
4. Could a relative keep the child and take them for regular visits? Can the children stay at the rehab for weekends?

The rehab house

1. What special provision does the house make for children – or do they just have a toy box in the corner?
2. Do they make special provision, when the parent and child first arrive, to help the child settle in?
3. Does the parent see the child regularly?
4. If the house is very structured in its organisation and therapy regime, is there leeway for the upset and confused child to see the mother as and when the child wants to?
5. If the parent is confined to the house for the first month, can the child get out to see grandparents, siblings, etc?
6. What reason is the child given for being there?
7. Are there other children of a similar age in the house?
8. What about school/nursery/crèche facilities? Are these in-house, or is the child encouraged to mix with other children from outside? What about the stigma for the child coming from a rehab house?
9. Would other residents have access to the child? (few houses will accept those with a history of violence or a serious psychiatric record).
10. Is it clear who has responsibility for the child?

For further details on residential rehabilitation services that accept children, contact SCODA (see Appendix 2 for details).

Section Three

Young people and drugs

CASE STUDY THREE

A brother and sister, Jay (10) and Kaye (13), are among a group of young people who are detained by police on a Sunday afternoon on grounds of breach of the peace The local neighbours had complained about a series of glue-sniffing incidents in the park which were causing a disturbance and alarm. Social services were contacted because the parents were not at home around the time of the arrest. It transpires they were at friends in a nearby home. Kaye is very quiet and refuses to talk, but Jay is forthcoming and a number of things he says are quite alarming.

It seems that the children are regularly allowed to play on their own all day on Sunday and most of the evening. Jay tells the social worker that his parents are doing crack, but if his dad finds out he's said anything he will 'beat the shit out of me'. The police do not want to pursue this, saying they are reluctant to take the word of a 10-year-old in this matter.

SOME POINTS FOR CONSIDERATION

The reason social services have become involved in this case is that there was no adult able to be at the police interview. It is essential that this is treated in a sensitive and measured way, including not ignoring what is being said by the children.

The immediate risk posed to the children is likely to be from the solvents themselves, and they may not be aware of the dangers. This needs to be addressed.

The fact that the children are apparently alone for such long periods of time also raises concern, and this needs to be discussed in a non-confrontational way with the family.

The allegation of Jay will need to be borne in mind when making more enquiries, and a balance struck between taking the matter seriously and not making immediate assumptions. It is unlikely that the parents will be forthcoming about any drug use, but there may be indications that help to build a picture about what is actually happening. Crack bingeing at the week-ends tends to be a group activity that usually becomes apparent after a period of time.

Problems with debt, mood swings, craving for the substance, and so on could develop over time. It may be that after initial enquiries are made, the situation will have to be monitored to check that the children are receiving adequate care and that things are not deteriorating.

The social work context – an overview

Any social worker in contact with young people is likely to come up against issues relating to drug and alcohol use from time to time, and as such, needs to be prepared to approach this topic with an open mind. It is reasonable to suppose that a high number of young people who come into contact with social services will use drugs at some point in their lives. In so doing they are acting in a similar way to other young people of their age. Generally this drug use is relatively unproblematic. In such instances it becomes important for professionals to see drug use in its cultural context, as one feature of many young people's lives, and not necessarily as a problem behaviour in itself. However, on occasions a young person's drug use will take on more harmful and questionable aspects requiring a thoughtful and appropriate professional response.

> *Many young people experiment with drugs, but only a proportion of these use them on a regular basis. Of these, a proportion may develop patterns of use that are associated with psycho-social or physical problems*
> **(HAS Report 1996 p42).**

Professional responses to young people's substance use vary enormously, ranging from the indifferent *'it's no problem'* to the panic responses of *'I can't deal with this, call in the experts'*. Commonly, drug use is an issue that workers sweep under the carpet and prefer not to address, perhaps because of fears about their inability to respond appropriately or because of simply being overwhelmed by so many other problems and priorities in a young person's life. It is useful for the professional to consider a young person's drug use in a holistic way, as one of many potentially 'problem' behaviours such as criminal activity, non-school attendance, and aggression, remembering that none of these behaviours will necessarily be considered as problematic by the young person themselves. It is also important to look at each case where a young person is using drugs individually and to assess needs and possible harm on this individual basis.

WAYS IN WHICH DRUG USE MAY ARISE AS AN ISSUE
Situations where a young person's drug or alcohol use is the primary concern

In these circumstances a young person's drug or alcohol use is considered to be sufficiently problematic, either by the young person themselves or more commonly by another professional, for a referral to social services to be made. This would require a careful and comprehensive assessment to ascertain the nature of the drug use, for whom it is a problem, the risk of harm to the young person and others (see assessment below). In such a case, additional advice or support from a professional with drug expertise might be useful. More commonly, however, problem drug use appears as one of a number of causes for concern.

SITUATIONS WHERE DRUG USE IS ONE OF A NUMBER OF PROBLEM ISSUES FOR THE YOUNG PERSON
Typically, a young person's drug use will not be easily isolated from a number of problematic and non-problematic teenage behaviours. Referrals are perhaps more likely to focus on a breakdown in family relationships, allegations of abuse or more general 'out of control' behaviour by a young person. Alternatively, a young person who is currently looked after by the local authority might be found to be using drugs to an extent which causes concern for residential workers or foster carers.

SITUATIONS WHERE DRUG USE IS NOT AN ISSUE
For many young people looked after by the local authority, drug and alcohol use will not be an issue of particular concern. However, it is worth bearing in mind that there is a strong likelihood that such young people will have missed opportunities for drug education and awareness

lessons which might be available in school, and they are particularly likely to be exposed to some level of risk. As such they will need access to good and timely advice and information from other sources.

The following chapters aim to provide social workers with basic information relating firstly to issues of young people's drug use – numbers, why they use, the legal background – to provide some perspective and context for this area of work. In addition, they begin to address some of the practice issues specific to social work with young drug users ranging from assessment, through possible responses, and on to referral.

How many young people use drugs?

DRUG USE BY YOUNG PEOPLE: PREVALENCE AND TRENDS

'While research data about substance use and misuse by children and adolescents in the UK is limited, certain trends are apparent and give cause for concern. These include:
- *the increased use of a wide range of drugs by the younger age group*
- *increasing use among girls*
- *the emergence of polydrug use as the norm*
- *lowering of the age of initiation into substance use.*

Adolescents are also growing up in a culture in which drugs are much more easily available, acceptable and their consumption more readily perceived as 'normal' within peer groups'

(HAS Report 1996 p7)

Drug use is essentially a young person's activity, with a spectrum of use which peaks at the end of the teenage years. Although one in four people may report the lifetime use of drugs, the 1994 British Crime Survey found that only 13 per cent of 45- to 59-year-olds but 46 per cent of 16- to 19-year-olds said they had taken drugs (Ramsey & Percy, 1996).

SCHOOLCHILDREN

In general, the school age population is still drug free, but contact with drugs and drug users is a daily occurrence. It is probably fair to say that around one in twelve 12-year-olds and one in three 14-year-olds will have tried drugs, and that by the time they take their GCSEs, around two in five schoolchildren will also have taken a drug (Baker, 1997).

The Exeter school surveys carried out annually by John Balding provide useful information here. Balding's studies consistently survey the largest number of schoolchildren in Britain – in 1992, 20,000; in 1993, 29,000; in 1994, 48,000; and in 1995, 18,000. The studies are not perfect – they are school-based and so may suffer from the probability that drug users are less likely than non-users to be in school when the survey is conducted. However, what they are able to do is present young people's perceptions of drug use, and activities relating to this.

In 1995, 9 per cent of 12- to 13-year-olds (Year 8 pupils) said that they had taken illegal drugs or solvents, rising to 30 per cent of 14- to 15-year-olds (Year 10) and 37 per cent of 15- to 16-year-olds (Year 11) (Balding, 1996). Looking back over the series of studies, the proportion of 12- to 13-year-olds which admitted to having used drugs in 1995 was greater than that of the 15- to 16-year-olds in 1987.

Drugs Futures, a regional study carried out by researchers from Manchester University over a three-year period in the early 1990s, was the first to find a general population's lifetime drug use top the 50 per cent mark for any age group – by the final year of research, 51 per cent of 16-year-olds said that they had taken drugs. The researchers concluded:

'Over the next few years, and certainly in urban areas, non-drug-trying adolescents will be a minority group. In one sense **they will be the deviants**. Professionals in education, health care and the criminal justice system, politicians and parents, urgently need to acknowledge that **for many young people taking drugs has become the norm.**' [Emphasis added.]

(Parker et al, 1995 p26).

Pulling together the results from all of these surveys, it is safe to say that across the United Kingdom as a whole – around one in twelve 12-year-olds, one in three 14-year-olds and two in five 16-year-olds will have tried drugs.

YOUNG ADULTS

The years between the end of compulsory schooling at 16 and the approach of middle age at around 35 are consistently found to be the peak periods for illegal drug use. Studies suggest that around one in two people in their late teens and early 20s will have used drugs and that around a third of these will still be using them (Baker, 1997). This level of current use seems to fall to one in four in the late 20s and to tail away to about one in ten thereafter.

GENDER

It is generally assumed that more men than women use drugs, but this is a far from simple assertion. Age plays an important role here. Marsden & Percy (1996) found that half of all men between 16 and 29 had taken drugs compared with only a third of women in the same age group. However, in the 16-19 age group, women were matching men's drug consumption almost drug for drug. As for under-16s, the Exeter school surveys have found that school age drug use is remarkable in its similarity between the sexes (Balding, 1995 and 1996).

CLASS

As with gender, there is an assumption that socio-economic status is in some way related to drug use. It almost certainly is, but it cannot yet be said whether such a relationship is causal or simply associative. Until recently the view held was that drug users are in general poor, unskilled or unemployed. However, recent surveys have called into question the validity of this view (Marsden & Percy, 1996). The reality is more complex – as a socio-economic group, professional and skilled workers were more likely to have taken drugs (and to continue taking them) but the drug use of unskilled workers was of a higher frequency using more dangerous methods of administration.

ETHNICITY

Most recent studies confirm that the pattern of drug use among ethnic groups is as diverse as among British whites (Marsden 1996, Leitner 1993). These surveys show that African Caribbean drug use is identical to that of British whites, although there does appear to be a pattern of hard drug use among young Asian people which has previously gone unnoticed.

Leitner's Four City Study (1993) found white and African Caribbean lifetime drug use to be identical, at 29 per cent, with Indian use standing at 11 per cent and Pakistani/Bangladeshi at 15 per cent. Although African Caribbeans aged between 30 and 59 had a higher rate of lifetime use than whites in the same age group (25 per cent compared with 22 per cent), their counterparts aged 16-29 had a rate of lifetime use which was substantially lower than that of whites – 34 per cent compared with 43 per cent. What does seem to be worrying in terms of ethnicity is the relatively high levels of use of certain drugs recorded by the British Crime Survey in the Pakistani/Bangladeshi communities (Marsden, 1996). Among 16- to 29-year-olds, 4 per cent of Pakistanis/Bangladeshis had taken heroin and 3 per cent crack, more than the other ethnic groups put together. In the same age group, 4 per cent had also taken cocaine (only 3 per cent of whites had) and 2 per cent steroids (only 1 per cent of whites had). Asian drug use has been a long-neglected area of study but the 1994 British Crime Survey seems to suggest that it has patterns of use which are peculiarly its own, thus meriting further study.

WHAT DO THEY TAKE?

The 1990s saw the most remarkable departure from earlier decades with the integration of LSD and ecstasy into mass youth culture. There also appears to have been a trend towards greater variety in drug use – towards polydrug use, with people growing ever more confident at matching their drug use to their mood, pocket and environment.

That said, cannabis is still the most common drug, taken by perhaps one in five of the population and by two in five young people. In general, the hallucinogenic and stimulant drugs will have been used by around one in ten young people – more specifically, about one in seven young people will have used amphetamines or LSD, one in ten magic mushrooms or amyl nitrite and around one in twelve will have tried ecstasy (Baker, 1997). Solvent use is difficult to gauge because of an apparent reluctance to report it, but it's likely that about one in ten teenagers will try it and unlikely that any other age groups will do so. Use of the drugs that most concern the British press and public – heroin, cocaine and crack – is recorded at low but measurable levels in the general population (around 1 or 2 per cent). Among young people, however, while heroin and crack use is still very low, the use of cocaine is considerably higher – perhaps 4 per cent of young people will have tried it. Overall trends suggest that less than 1 per cent will ever have injected a drug (Baker, 1997).

Why do young people use drugs?

Social work professionals are often keen to understand the reasons for a particular behaviour and numerous commentators have sought to list and explore the reasons behind young people's drug use. When young people themselves are asked why they take drugs, common responses include 'to escape reality', 'to relax', 'because I enjoy them' – not dissimilar to adults' reasons for drinking alcohol. This perspective on drugs as pleasurable – more often than not young people enjoy the experience of taking ecstasy or smoking cannabis – needs to be taken seriously by professionals. Richard Ives (1995) gives a fairly pragmatic list of reasons why young people might use solvents, in summary they are:

- drugs can be fun, a pleasant activity, especially with a group of friends
- some young people like the excitement of drug use, perhaps partly because of the element of danger
- if adults are shocked by drug use, that can be an attraction
- for some young people there is the attraction of playing with a new physical sensation
- some use drugs because their friends are trying them
- others use them to blot out problems
- others to help them cope with difficult social and emotional situations.

Below, a number of commonly cited 'reasons' are set out in more detail.

YOUTH CULTURE/SUBCULTURES

The concept of youth culture has evolved around the increasing independence, leisure time and spending power of young people. In the 1990s drugs have been increasingly absorbed into the mainstream youth culture, with the growth in the use of certain drugs such as ecstasy, LSD and amphetamines associated with staying awake and dancing at all night 'raves'.

Nowadays drug use, especially cannabis, is an integral part of the youth consumer market interwoven with music and fashion. While subcultural theorists have focused their attention on some of the more notorious and colourful youth subcultures of the past 40 years, such as hippies, mods and punks, there is also a mass of 'ordinary' young people whose essential routine concerns are school, home and employment. They may adopt the demeanour, fashion and slang of a particular subculture including the occasional or experimental use of illegal drugs without necessarily adopting the lifestyle. In fact, the majority of young people's drug use is restricted to the use of tobacco and alcohol: for many the pub is the centre of community life.

Overall, the evidence of drug use within youth culture suggests that the experience of substances is often pleasurable rather than negative and damaging. The use of drugs such as cannabis and LSD is often looked back on with fondness rather than regret by the now middle aged who were once active participants. The understanding of the cultural role and purpose of drug use will help in the planning of effective and realistic programmes of education on drugs.

ENVIRONMENT

Many young people live in communities which suffer from multiple deprivation, with high unemployment and low quality housing where the surrounding infra-structure of local services is fractured and poorly resourced. In such communities drug supply and use often thrive as an alternative economy often controlled by powerful criminal groups. As well as any use that might be associated with the stress and boredom of living in such communities, young people with poor job prospects recognise the financial advantages and the status achievable through the business of small scale supply of drugs.

However, drug use is certainly not restricted only to areas of urban deprivation. As the press stories of expulsions from private schools show, illicit drug use is an aspect of the whole of our society.

CURIOSITY

Most young people are naturally curious and want to experiment with different experiences. For some, drugs are a good conversation point – they are interesting to talk about and fascinate everyone.

THE DEFENCE MECHANISM

Some young people will use drugs specifically to ease the trauma and pain of unsatisfactory relationships and the physical and emotional abuse arising from unhappy home lives. They will often come to the attention of statutory authorities, whether through school, social services referrals or the criminal justice system. If these other problems are satisfactorily addressed, then it is possible that drug use may become less of a problem.

NATURAL REBELLION

Whether or not part of any particular subset of youth culture, young people like to be exclusive, own something that is personal to themselves and consciously or unconsciously drug use may act as a means of defiance to provoke adults into a reaction.

PROMOTION AND AVAILABILITY

There is considerable pressure to use legal substances – alcohol and pain-relieving drugs are regularly advertised on television. Despite legislation, children and teenagers have no problems obtaining alcohol and tobacco from any number of retail outlets; breweries refurbish pubs with young people in mind, bringing in music, games, more-sophisticated décor and so on, while the general acceptance of these drugs is maintained through sports sponsorship, promotions and other marketing strategies. Obviously, the illicit market is more discreet, but in circumstances where illegal drugs are available, the demand for and use of these substances by young people will increase.

COST

Value for money is often a factor as to which drug to use. At the time of writing, cannabis sufficient for a few joints would cost about £5, while an LSD trip would be around £2.50. In terms of how long the effects last, this compares very favourably with an average price for a pint of lager of around £1.80. By the same token, ecstasy of highly variable quality is still selling for £10-15 a tablet and many drug users have been voting with their wallet and turning to cheaper drugs such as LSD and amphetamines.

RISK AND PROTECTIVE FACTORS

An alternative way of explaining drug use considers risk factors, which can be categorised into two main groups: societal and cultural factors which provide the normative social expectations, and individual and interpersonal factors. Alongside these, there is increasing interest in protective factors as variables in their own right. Following this analysis, prevention strategies would ideally target vulnerable groups of young people, reducing the multiple risks they experience and enhancing the protective factors.

SUMMARY OF RISK AND PROTECTIVE FACTORS ASSOCIATED WITH PROBLEM DRUG USE:

Societal and Cultural Risk Factors

The law and societal norms	Extreme economic deprivation
Substance availability	Neighbourhood disorganisation

Individual and Interpersonal Risk Factors

Physiological	Academic problems
Family attitudes to substance use or misuse	Low commitment to school
	Early peer rejection
Use of substances by parents	Association with peers who use drugs
Poor and inconsistent family management practices	Alienation
	Attitudes favourable to drug use
Family conflict	Early onset of drug or alcohol use
Early and persistent behaviour problems	

Protective Factors

Positive temperament	A social support system that
Intellectual ability	encourages personal efforts
A supportive family environment	A caring relationship with at least one adult

(HAS Report 1996 p28)

Legal considerations

Nobody below 10 years of age in England and Wales, or eight in Scotland, can be convicted of a criminal offence.

MISUSE OF DRUGS ACT 1971

This Act aims to prevent the unauthorised possession and distribution of a wide range of drugs without prescription. Surprisingly, the Act does not actually outlaw the use of drugs. However, it does create offences including:

- possession (simply having the drug)
- possession with intent to supply the drug to another person
- production (including cultivation)
- supplying or offering to supply another person
- import or export.
- allowing premises that you occupy or manage to be used for supplying drugs.

SOLVENTS

It is not an offence to have or to sniff glues, solvents, or gases, such as lighter refills or aerosols.

Under Scottish law, young people below 16 found sniffing solvents can be referred to the Reporter of the Children's Panel and may (if a hearing thinks it is in the best interests of the child) be taken into care.

THE CHILDREN ACT 1989

There is no specific mention of young people's substance misuse under the Children Act except for a general mention under 'medical requirements'. Part 3 of the Act relates to the powers of local authorities in respect of children in need and the protection of children suffering or likely to suffer harm. The needs of young people with problem drug and alcohol use are generally regarded as falling within these definitions. Some local authorities include the children of drug-using parents as in need, although this certainly does not mean they automatically need to be looked after by the local authority. A number of principles contained in the Act underpin all work with young people:

- that the welfare of the child is the paramount consideration in court proceedings
- that children should be kept informed about what happens to them and should participate when decisions are made about their future
- that services should meet each child's identified needs
- that services should be appropriate to each child's race, culture, religion and language.

As a rule, all social work intervention with young drug users that has a child protection element will necessarily require a worker to adhere to the locally agreed area child protection committee guidelines.

CHILDREN IN NEED

Part 3 of the Act details a local authority's general duty to provide a range of services to children in their area who are 'in need'. While definitions vary locally, most local authorities include children with drug-, alcohol- or solvent-dependency problems as children 'in need' and therefore entitled to a priority in the provision of services following assessment or investigation. Some local authorities also prioritise children whose parents use drugs or alcohol in such a way as to seriously impair their parenting.

UNDER 16S

At the time of writing, there are no formally agreed guidelines as to legally acceptable and appropriate ways of giving harm-minimisation advice and services to drug users aged under 16. The particular concern here is how to responsibly and effectively meet the needs of young opiate users and young injectors without putting drug agencies and workers at risk of prosecution. To date, some services have been applying the Gillick principle to their work with young drug users.

In the Gillick case it was held that a doctor could legally

prescribe contraception for a girl under 16 without the consent of her parents, with a number of preconditions:

> 1) that the young person will understand the advice
> 2) that the young person cannot be persuaded to inform his or her parents or allow them to be informed that the young person is seeking drug advice or treatment in respect of substance use
> 3) that the young person is very likely to begin or continue using substances with or without the advice or treatment
> 4) that, unless the young person receives advice or treatment on the use of substances, his or her physical or mental health or both are likely to suffer; and
> 5) that the young person's best interests require the adviser to give advice and/or treatment without parental consent.
>
> **(HAS Report 1996 p95)**

SCODA's Young People and Drugs good practice unit are exploring this area of practice – see Appendix 2 for contact details.

CONFIDENTIAL DISCLOSURES BY YOUNG PEOPLE

When it comes to discussing drug use, it is important that young people feel their right to confidentiality is respected. There is no legal requirement to report a criminal offence to the police, except in Northern Ireland (Criminal Law Act 1967); however, it is important for professionals to consult their own agency guidelines on this issue as some local authorities do recommend informing the police in certain circumstances, such as cases of supplying drugs.

The National Foster Care Association (NFCA,1991) takes the view that, unlike natural parents, foster carers have little right of discretion and should inform someone, either the police or local authority, of a young person's drug use.

It is important for social workers to be clear with young people from the outset what information needs to be shared with others (and with whom). Particular sensitivity is needed in cases where young people want information on drug use kept confidential from their parents. Ideally, in the spirit of the Children Act, young people disclosing drug use should be encouraged to share any problems with their parents. When the facts are unclear, however, many local authorities discourage the passing on of rumours or suspicions to parents.

Clearly the safety of the young person and others will be a worker's prime consideration, so there may be occasions when information will have to be passed on in line with boundaries of confidentiality. This may include circumstances where:

- the child is at risk of significant harm if disclosure is not made
- there is a legal requirement for the information to be disclosed
- public interest requires disclosure in order to prevent others being put at risk.

It is worth bearing in mind that other agencies have quite different policies on confidentiality. There is much potential for conflict here among multi-agency partnerships, for example among health workers/voluntary agencies/social workers if they are not all clear from the outset on their individual agency definitions and the appropriate level of information sharing needed among themselves.

Assessment

More often than not a social worker will engage in an informal and rapid information gathering operation as regards a young person's drug use rather than a more formal assessment. This information gathering will involve talking with the young person themselves, maybe their carers and other concerned adults and professionals. For social workers, it is important to address young people's drug use in partnership with the full range of generic and specialist youth and health agencies.

To quote the HAS (1996), *'No-one should work with young people in isolation.'* p108. Once a need for further exploration has been decided upon, it is important that some care is given to the assessment process. Before starting, it is important for the worker to be clear what the problem actually is, why it is a problem, and who has defined it? Also to be on the look-out for a mismatch between adults' and young persons' perceptions. Workers need to remember that drug use does not necessarily lead to problems for young people.

Forms of drug use

Drug use is often broken down in the following ways:

Experimental use – This tends to be short term. Usually a group activity. Exploratory choice of substance, method of use and situation. May be the first time. May be ill-informed, novice use, lacking in knowledge and information.

Recreational use – Usually medium or longer term. Usually a group activity. This is controlled use where knowledge of norms of use are established. Tends to be specific in terms of choice of substance, circumstances and method of use, for example evening drinking or use of ecstasy at raves at weekends.

Dependent use – This is often longer term and may well be a solitary or small-group activity. May be either discriminating or undiscriminating in choice of substance, method of use, or circumstances.

Knowledge of these different types of use can help the worker to improve their understanding as to why a young person is using drugs and what the most appropriate responses might be. The majority of users fall within the experimental and recreational categories; however, these are not exclusive categories and a young person's pattern of use may change over time. Problems may occur with any of these types of use but the nature of them and their solutions may be different.

All social work teams should have guidelines for their staff on the assessment and care management of young drug users. Such guidelines need to be drawn up and agreed with the Area Child Protection Committee.

ASSESSING THE NEEDS OF A YOUNG PERSON – SOME CONSIDERATIONS

There is a difficult balance to be achieved by an assessor who needs to avoid focusing too much on the young person's drug use to the extent that other needs and issues are lost, but must not take such a general or holistic approach that drug and alcohol problems are not satisfactorily addressed. Ideally, all social service assessments will include a section on use of drugs and alcohol so these issues become addressed routinely and as a matter of course. In reality, detailed exploration of substance use is most likely to take place when problems have been flagged up either by young people themselves or by others. Agency guidelines on assessing children and young people should be used whenever appropriate and it is important to bear in mind that, where possible child protection issues arise, workers will need to follow the locally agreed Area Child Protection Committee procedures.

Assessments will need to cover the problems, the needs and the requirements for intervention, treatment or care of the young person. The assessment of some problems necessitates the involvement of other agencies because of their complexity. In addition there will need to be consideration of the young person's competence, capabilities and development. 'Grilling' young people about their drug use will inevitably prove ineffective; however, there may be occasions when the accuracy of information provided by the young person will need to be considered and, if appropriate, the truthfulness cross-checked with others.

ASSESSING A YOUNG PERSON'S DRUG USE

There follows a list of questions which may be used to assess the type of drug use young persons are engaging in:

- *what drug/s are they using?*
- *how much of the drug?*
- *how often are they using?*
- *are they mixing drugs? or drugs and alcohol?*
- *what methods are being used to take the drug? For example, smoking/injecting/sniffing*
- *how long have they been using?*
- *who else, if anyone, is involved?*
- *where does use take place?*
- *how is the use being funded?*
- *how much does the user know about drug use?*
- *how does the user feel about their use?*

ASSESSING THE RISKS AND EFFECTS OF DRUG USE

Drug and alcohol use may prove to be unproblematic for young persons in as much as they are experiencing no adverse effects from their use, no health, legal or social problems. As stated above much of young people's drug use is considered and controlled. For example, a young woman who takes an amphetamine at the occasional party does run certain risks, namely, the drug may be of low purity, she might get arrested for possession – but in the absence of such occurrences she may well see her drug use in terms of an occasional 'treat' rather than a problem.

At the other end of the scale, a young person may be using drugs chaotically in such a way that the use is deeply enmeshed (cause and effect) in a problem lifestyle. For example, the young solvent sniffer who uses glue, aerosols, lighter fuel, whatever he can get his hands on to get 'out of it'. His health is poor, he has been expelled from school as a result of poor attendance, lack of concentration and erratic behaviour, his social relationships are limited. Lots of problems for this young man, some perhaps causing, some perhaps resulting from, his solvent use.

The following summary lists possible risks and problems of drug use to bear in mind when working with young people.

HEALTH RISKS

These can involve a range of physical and psychological effects associated with drug use, including the short-term health risks associated with use of a particular drug or mix of drugs, for example, paranoia linked with a bad LSD trip, or nausea and unconsciousness caused by too much alcohol. They also include long-term effects of use of a drug(s) over a prolonged period, for example, increased risks of abscesses associated with regular injecting in one site, and of those associated with contracting hepatitis or HIV through sharing contaminated injecting equipment. Alcohol and drug use are also significant risk factors for both suicide and deliberate self-harm. (See Appendix 1 for more details of risks associated with individual drugs.)

LEGAL RISKS

There is a range of legal restrictions relating to psychoactive drugs and unwanted risks associated with drug use. This includes the possibility of arrest or caution for possession or supply of illegal substances. Police forces vary in the severity of their response to small amounts of drugs found in someone's possession. However, penalties for those convicted of supplying substances (and this can be interpreted as just buying a couple of ecstasy tablets for yourself and a friend) can be heavy. The class of the drug, the amount, circumstances, and previous convictions will all play a part in response. (See Appendix 1 for details of individual drug classification.)

LIFESTYLE/SOCIAL RISKS

These may take the form of a breakdown in family or social relationships resulting from drug use. Alternatively they may manifest themselves as problems with authority or trouble with finances and accommodation. It needs to be remembered, however, that for many young people drug use is in itself a social activity and closely bound in with certain social settings – for example, ecstasy and the dance scene.

Responding to young people's drug use

If a young person arrives at an agency in a state of intoxification which is potentially life threatening, workers clearly need to take responsibility and call an ambulance so that medical help can be given. The comments given below relate primarily to non-crisis situations.

Depending on their assessment of the young person's drug use, the worker will have various options open to them. These may include:

1) Doing nothing
2) Exploring in more depth with the young person their drug use or associated issues and concerns – either informally, through keeping the channels of communication open and encouraging discussion, or perhaps more formally through regular counselling
3) Undertaking some form of education or prevention activity. This might include helping a young person maintain a drug-free lifestyle
4) Providing advice and information or initiating some intervention aimed at minimising the harm related to the use of a substance
5) Providing continued support for a young person, practical or emotional, in spite of their drug use or until such a time as they are ready to consider making changes
6) Convening a Child Protection Case Conference – if the possibility of the young person causing significant harm to themselves or to others arises
7) Refer the young person to another service where they can receive care, treatment or support for their drug use.

The options listed above are neither exhaustive nor mutually exclusive.

DOING NOTHING

Choosing not to act after an assessment or detailed information-gathering exercise is a valid option open to professional workers. There are good reasons why it may be appropriate not to make an issue of drugs or intervene in relation to a young person's use of drugs. If you know that another professional is adequately addressing the subject with the young person, for example, or if you have had a frank talk with her/him and you are sufficiently reassured that the young person is aware of potential risks, is managing these and in no immediate danger is one such hypothesis. Choosing not to act immediately may be about focusing on more pressing concerns, for example, a disclosure of abuse and waiting until events have settled down to talk through drug use issues that do not appear to be high risk.

DETAILED EXPLORATION

There will be times when a worker needs more information on a young person's drug use before deciding whether or not to intervene. Perhaps they need to consult with other professionals with knowledge of the young person, or maybe make an informal call to someone with drug 'expertise'. Perhaps they require more time to develop a trusting relationship with the young person, or to create a safe space for honest and open discussion. In such circumstances real incidents can be used as a spring-board to start off discussion or TV programmes used to prompt debate. The emphasis here is on maintaining a non-judgemental environment and keeping the channels of communication open so that a young person feels able to discuss any fears or concerns they might have. In some circumstances it might make sense to set up more formal counselling sessions to discuss problems more confidentially.

Whatever the circumstances, whether following up an incident, helping a young person give up drugs or discussing safer drug use, keep the focus on the young person rather than the drugs and beware of moralising.

EDUCATIONAL AND PREVENTION INTERVENTIONS

Social workers have a health promotion responsibility as

regards drug and alcohol use by young people –
particularly for those in residential care and supported
accommodation, as well as for young offenders. Looked
after or accommodated young people are among the most
vulnerable in terms of their likelihood of developing drug-
or alcohol-use problems at some stage in their lives.
Anecdotal evidence from drug agencies testifies to a high
proportion of adult drug users having been in local
authority care at some stage. What this indicates is an
increased need for effective drug education and
prevention work targeted on this particular client group.

The 'looked after' are probably among the least likely
groups of young people to receive formal drug and alcohol
input, largely because they spend so much of their young
lives outside of the mainstream structures – schools, youth
clubs – where a somewhat scant drug education may be
found. High levels of non-school-attendance among this
group can result in insufficient and often no input for
young people who are already at a higher- than-average
risk of problem use. As a consequence, a social worker
may represent a vital (sometimes the only) source of
accurate drugs information to a young person looked after
by the local authority.

Approaches to education

Factual approaches – such as the provision of information about
drug use and the effects.

Effective approaches – aims to increase awareness, coping and
decision- making skills.

Situational approaches – these take into account the social
factors that can influence an individual's decision making in
certain situations.

Cultural approaches – these use the context of people's lives as
a starting point from which to approach drug-use issues and
include the teaching of 'life skills'.

Reviews of the effectiveness of drug education
programmes indicate the limitations of their impact. What
is shown is that it is easier to improve knowledge than to
affect attitudes, and that sustained behaviour change is the
most difficult to achieve. Research suggests that effective

education and prevention interventions should be multi-focal in:

- encouraging individual responsibility
- involving young people in planning and implementing programmes
- encouraging peer support
- recruiting adult teachers and workers who are open, supportive and non-judgemental

(HAS Report, 1996)

In summary, drug prevention interventions need to be targeted and educators need to receive training. Drug education for young people being looked after by the local authority might usefully be considered alongside sex education and HIV prevention. (Organisations such as TACADE provide training and materials in drug education and prevention. SCODA has produced a directory of education and prevention initiatives across the country. Local drug prevention teams may also offer support and training. See Appendix 2 for contact details.)

Children and young people for whom the local authority are providing services may also be particularly at risk of HIV infection, for example because of injecting drug misuse or involvement in prostitution, and thought should be given as to how basic HIV prevention work can be integrated into services.

(Children and HIV – guidance for local authorities Dept. of Health, 1992. p22)

MINIMISING HARM – SAFER DRUG USE

'The working party recognise in accord with the Children Act 1989, that 'the child's welfare is paramount'. There is, therefore, a clear need for services to accept that for some children drug misuse may be a part of their life and there is also a need to recognise the importance of harm minimisation strategies. This may be for some a clear departure from what has been previously accepted'
(Northern Drug Services Child Care Groups, Under 16s Working Party, 1991 p22).

Professionals working with young drug users find themselves barraged by numerous contradictory pressures which, if they are not careful, can result in risky or ineffective responses. At a professional level they need to work within the law and not be seen to in any way encourage or condone the use of illegal substances. Simultaneously they are required to respond realistically and non-judgementally and above all in a way that prioritises the welfare of the young person.

If a young person refuses to stop using drugs, one of the few options open to a professional might be to try and persuade them to cut down on particularly risky behaviours. These safer-drug-use or harm-minimisation interventions with young people aim to educate and assist them in lessening the risks they take and the possible harm they may cause themselves. Such interventions may include provision of equipment, such as clean needles, or information on less risky ways of using substances. Social workers need to bear in mind, however, that provision of services to under 16s is currently a legally fraught area. (As previously mentioned, SCODA are working in this area, see Appendix 2 for contact details.)

While acknowledging the goal of dissuading young people from using drugs, the following list contains some points about safer ways of taking them:

- don't mix drugs, the effects can be unpredictable
- don't take drugs alone, ensure you are with someone in case you get in to trouble
- make sure drugs are taken in a safe place
- make sure you are calm and not wound up
- know what you are taking and from whom you got it
- know your limits, don't be pressurised into taking more than you can cope with
- be patient, drugs may take time to take effect, so don't overdose at the start
- if you are trying a drug for the first time, take a little to check it doesn't disagree with you
- if injecting, use clean needles and don't share injecting equipment
- if taking dance drugs drink small amounts of water regularly
- if taking solvents, use glue rather than aerosols
- carry a condom – if you have sex when stoned, take care of yourself.

CONTINUED SUPPORT

A key tool for a professional working with a young person is the therapeutic relationship with the client. This is as true with drug use as for any other issue – such as abuse or bereavement – and through counselling and the exchange of information the young person can be assisted to recognise whether or not they have a problem and, if so, how to act.

CHILD PROTECTION

'Statutory powers only exist to offer a young person protection from self harm when a seriously life threatening situation has arisen and clearly defined conditions can be met to satisfy a court.'
(Tameside Social Services, 1992 p4).

'We do not believe that young people indulging in injection or under age sex should automatically be placed on a child protection register or automatically have their parents informed. Instead, practitioners should encourage young people to have dialogue with their parents and, if needs be, and with the client's consent, facilitate that dialogue'
(Northern Drug Services, 1991 p22).

Clearly, a young person's problem drug or alcohol use in itself is no reason for local authority child protection machinery to swing into action. However, there will be occasions when a young person is considered to be at risk of causing significant harm to themselves or others. In this situation, a case conference needs to be convened and options including placing the young person's name on the Child Protection register, considered. In all cases, procedures laid down by the local Area Child Protection Committee need to be followed.

YOUNG PEOPLE ACCOMMODATED BY THE LOCAL AUTHORITY

Frontline workers such as residential workers and foster carers are most likely to be put in the position of having to deal with 'crisis' situations such as someone collapsing after bingeing on a mixture of drugs or a young person being arrested for possession of amphetamines. These workers are most likely to walk into a room where young people are smoking cannabis or be told about someone's heroin use by a friend. They may have to deal with disposal of illegal substances as well as staying with a young person who is coming down off alcohol or drugs.

Similarly these workers will need to consider health and safety issues in relation to their premises – ensuring all 'abusable' substances are locked away. (See *DrugsCare*, 1996, for detailed advice here). There may be slightly different issues for foster carers as regards drug use and looked after young people. For a start, use may take place in the context of the foster carer's family – they may have particular fears about the effects on members of their own family. NFCA guidelines oblige foster carers to inform social services departments about any drug use by a young person in their care.

PARENTS OF YOUNG DRUG-USERS

Social workers may find themselves working with parents of young drug-users. The situation calls for sensitive handling because parental over-reaction in cases of a young person experimenting could do a lot of damage. Both the social worker and parent need to acknowledge that, in most cases, experimentation will not result in increased drug use.

In circumstances where a young person has drug dependency problems, parents can feel a sense of failure and find it difficult to acknowledge the truth. In such circumstances, referral to a local support group or telephone help line (where these exist) might provide a useful source of support (ADFAM have a phone line for families of drug users, see Appendix 2 for details).

REFERRAL

There may be occasions where the social worker considers it appropriate to refer a young drug-user to another agency. Before a referral is made, a number of factors will need to be thought through:

- why is a referral needed? What can the service offer that the worker can't? The truth is that few specialist agencies have experience of working with under 16s as most were set up to cater for adult opiate users. More often than not the social worker will be closer to the young person and better placed to help them

- does the young person want to be referred? A worker might wish to contact a specialist drug agency for advice or information, even if the young person does not wish to be referred
- is it the right time for a referral? Referring too early can push someone further down the line towards the drug problems the original referral was intended to address. Referring too early may result in a young person being labelled as someone with a drug problem, plus there is the risk of putting them in contact with older and more 'committed' drug users
- does the young person understand what the service offers, in terms of its ways of working, its confidentiality policies, etc?
- what continued support would be available for the young person both during and as follow up to a referral?

If, after consideration, referral to a specialist service appears to be the most appropriate option for meeting a young person's needs (and sometimes it is), then it is a case of finding out what is available. This may prove to be more difficult than it seems, as generally there is very little provision for the young drug-user.

Service Options

Services for drug and alcohol users tend to be aimed at the older, more entrenched user. A 1996 review of drug treatment services for young people painted a gloomy picture. It showed that:

- generally there is lack of recognition by professionals of the needs arising from substance use by young people
- specialised treatment for young people in England and Wales is extremely limited
- some young people are less likely to gain access to services than others. They include the homeless, those living in rural areas, and young people with multiple problems
- under 17s are not usually admitted to inpatient facilities for detoxification

(HAS Report, 1996)

So what services are available for the under 18s? In two words, very few. Below we list possible service options, though they are thinly spread and seemingly randomly situated.

ADULT DRUG SERVICES

Some adult services do see young people over the age of 16. A few have employed a nominated young persons worker or set up a young persons team within the agency. Overall, however, relatively few adult drug workers are trained, fully competent or sufficiently legally protected to work with under 16s.

COMMUNITY SERVICES

A range of generic, statutory and voluntary services exist in local areas – for example, advice and information agencies, counselling services, helplines, all offering interventions which might be of use to young drug users. More specialised community services exist such as outreach projects, health promotion organisations, and needle exchanges.

CHILD AND ADOLESCENT MENTAL HEALTH SERVICES (CAMHS)

Child and adolescent mental health services work with young people with a range of problems, where drug use is just one concern among others. The HAS (1996) found that most CAMHS do not see young people who present with substance misuse as a primary problem.

INPATIENT FACILITIES

Detoxification facilities do not usually admit young people under the age of 17 and many adolescent inpatient psychiatric units have drug or alcohol use as an exclusion criterion.

RESIDENTIAL REHABS

Almost all residential rehabs have a lower age limit of 18. Just a few take those aged 16-plus. There is an absence of rehab provision for under 16s. SCODA has identified only one residential establishment that takes 11- to 17- year-olds: Middlegate Lodge in Lincolnshire (SCODA, 1997).

GETTING HELP AROUND REFERRALS

For an overview of what local services exist that might offer help to young drug-users, it is worth contacting your local social services or health authority commissioner with a responsibility for drug services. Alternatively you might try to get hold of your Drug Action Team co-ordinator (many of these are based in the health authority) for information or contacts.

At a national level, SCODA produce a directory of drug agencies across the country with details on age restrictions. The National Children's Bureau (Solvent Misuse Project) produce a directory of residential projects for young people, with details on which ones admit solvent, alcohol and drug users.

Appendix 1: Drugs – a brief guide

ALCOHOL

A depressant drug, consisting largely of water and ethanol, drunk by over 90 per cent of the adult population to a greater or lesser extent. Generally associated with socialising and relaxation.

SHORT-TERM EFFECTS

Effects start within five or ten minutes. The effect of a alcoholic drink depends on such factors as strength, how quickly it is drunk, food in the stomach, body weight and personality. A drinker tends to feel less inhibited and more relaxed after the equivalent of about two pints of beer. In high doses there can be drunken behaviour, drowsiness and stupor. If taken at the same time as other depressant drugs it will result in an exaggerated effect on the nervous system. Lasts several hours, depending on dose.

LONG-TERM EFFECTS

Individuals become 'alcoholic' after substantial tolerance has developed. Heavy drinking encourages obesity which may be accompanied by dietary deficiencies. Stomach and liver disorders can occur, resulting in incapacitating brain damage. Women who drink heavily while pregnant may give birth to babies with withdrawal symptoms, facial abnormalities or development problems.

LAW

There is no law against possessing or drinking alcohol, except that, under the Public Order Act 1986, it is an offence to carry or possess alcohol on public transport travelling to and from designated sporting events.

OTHER NAMES/SLANG

Beer, lager, wine, whisky, spirits, booze etc.

AMPHETAMINES

**Stimulant drug. Usually sniffed as a powder, dabbed
and taken orally or injected. Makes people more
awake and lively. Lasts several hours.**

SHORT-TERM EFFECTS

Raised heartbeat and blood pressure. Reduces appetite
and tiredness. Tiredness felt when effects wear off.

LONG-TERM EFFECTS

Ill health due to lack of food and sleep. Calcium deficiency
causing dental problems. Chronic use can lead to anxiety
or acute paranoia and psychosis.

LAW

Controlled under Misuse of Drugs Act (hereafter MDA).
Illegal to have unless prescribed by a doctor. Illegal to sell
or give away.

SLANG

Billy, whizz, speed, sulph, sulphate.

ALKYL NITRATES

**Stimulant-like drugs; amyl, butyl and –butyl nitrite.
Sold in small bottles. Used to enhance sexual
pleasure; general 'high'.**

SHORT-TERM EFFECTS

Instant 'rush' to the brain lasting two to five minutes, rapid
heartbeat, headache, relaxed muscles, nausea, weakness.

LONG-TERM EFFECTS

Generally none; however, a few fatalities caused by users
swallowing liquid.

LAW

Controlled under the Medicines Act (hereafter MA). Not
illegal to possess.

SLANG

Poppers.

Anabolic steroids

A stimulant-like drug derived from male hormone. Swallowed as a pill or capsule and also injected. Used by some athletes and body-builders to increase muscle size and aggression.

Short-term effects

Users report that the drugs make them feel more aggressive and so they train harder and also recover from injury more quickly.

Long-term effects

Used over a long period of time (which has to be done for anything to happen), these drugs affect men and women in different ways.

Women may become more 'masculine' (for example, deeper voice and smaller breasts) and these effects may not be reversible, even after use of the drugs has ceased.

In men, the reproductive system may be temporarily affected. Typical pattern of acne across back and shoulders. Possible development of breast tissue as body tries to compensate for presence of too much male hormone. For the same reason, some reports of so-called 'roid rage'. May be a factor in some instances of domestic violence where there is a steroid using body-builder in the family.

Young people using these drugs regularly over a period of time, may stunt their growth. In rare cases, users have died of liver cancer caused by steroids.

Law

Controlled under MDA, but only for supply, not possession.

Benzodiazopines

Minor tranquillisers and hypnotics, benzodiazepines are depressants which tend to be used to relieve anxiety and promote sleep in insomniacs.

Short-term effects

Depress mental activity and alertness, relieving tension and anxiety. Some people feel drowsy and lethargic, which initially may impair driving and similar skills. Side-effects that fade after a week or two of continuous use. In non-anxious individuals benzodiazepines do not generally produce positive feelings of pleasure or well-being.

LONG-TERM EFFECTS
Ineffective against anxiety and insomnia after four months of use. After a year or more individuals take benzodiazepines more because of dependence rather than the drug being still medically effective. A dependence mainly psychological in nature.

LAW
Controlled under Class C of the Misuse of Drugs Act, which makes it illegal to supply them. Prescription Only under the Medicines Act.

OTHER NAMES/SLANG
Valium, librium, ativan, benzos, tranx.

CANNABIS
Comes mainly in the form of leaves or resin. Smoked in a cigarette or pipe, by itself or with tobacco. Can be eaten.

SHORT-TERM EFFECTS
Usually makes people feel relaxed and talkative. If someone's anxious or depressed, it could make them feel worse. Makes people more sensitive to sounds and colours. Lasts 20 minutes to several hours. Makes concentration and quick reactions difficult.

LONG-TERM EFFECTS
Possible lung damage and other respiratory problems if smoked. Stronger varieties of cannabis (eg 'skunk',) could cause more LSD-like effects (see below).

LAW
Controlled under the MDA. Illegal to have, to sell, or give away.

SLANG
Dope, puff, weed, blow, draw, blunts, smoke, spliff, hash.

COCAINE AND CRACK

Stimulant drug. White powder or small raisin-sized crystal (crack). Sniffed or injected (cocaine powder) or smoked (crack).

SHORT-TERM EFFECTS

Very similar to amphetamines, except that cocaine only lasts for up to half an hour and crack wears off even quicker and the feelings with both are much more intense.

LONG-TERM EFFECTS

Strong possibility of dependency with regular chronic use. Such users may exhibit acute anxiety and paranoia. Crack use associated with domestic violence, sexual abuse of women.

LAW

Controlled under the MDA. Illegal to have, to sell or give away.

SLANG

Charlie, coke (cocaine); rock, stones (crack).

ECSTASY (TECHNICALLY KNOWN AS MDMA)

Stimulant drug. Swallowed as a pill or capsule.

SHORT-TERM EFFECTS

Raises temperature, sweating, raised heartbeat and blood pressure. Users report feeling very energetic and empathetic with those around them. In higher doses, some of the effects of amphetamine 'kick in', such as anxiety.

Fatalities associated with effects of the drug linked to the environment of dance clubs.

LONG-TERM EFFECTS

If used repeatedly, person may become anxious, panicky confused or depressed. Evidence of liver damage.

LAW

Controlled under the MDA. Illegal to have, to sell, or give away.

E, plus many others based on the colours and shapes of
the capsules and the markings on them, eg doves.

HEROIN

**An opiate drug. White powder which can be
swallowed, injected, sniffed or smoked. Small
amount makes people relaxed and content. Large
amount causes sleep. Stops pain. Lasts several hours.**

SHORT-TERM EFFECTS

Can make people feel sick. Makes concentration and quick
reactions difficult. Generally warm, drowsy feeling. Danger
of overdosing if injecting.

LONG-TERM EFFECTS

Reduced sex drive, problems with digestive system.
Damage to veins and skin and risk of infections like HIV
and hepatitis if injected. Easy to become dependent with
regular use. Withdrawal effects can be very unpleasant.

LAW

Illegal to have unless prescribed by a doctor. Illegal to sell
or give away.

SLANG

Junk, smack, skag, H, brown, nubain.
    Other opiates include methadone, temgesic, palfium,
codeine, diconal.

LSD

**Hallucinogenic drug. Swallowed as a liquid on
blotting paper.**

SHORT-TERM EFFECTS

Very dependent on situation and mood. Can make things
look and sound very different, and make people feel very
differently about themselves and about the world in
general. Lasts for eight to twelve hours and cannot be
stopped once the 'trip' is under way. Some may experience
a 'bad trip' and become anxious and frightened.

Long-term effects

Some users have a 'flashback' to the drug experience long after using the drug and without taking it again. LSD may 'trigger' a latent mental disorder.

Law

Controlled under the MDA. Illegal to have, to sell or to give away.

Slang

Acid, trips.

Solvents

Glues, aerosols and gases (like lighter fuel) the fumes of which can be inhaled to get 'high'.

Short-term effects

Lasts about half an hour. Like being very drunk. Risk of accidents and death (like vomiting while unconscious). Gases (aerosols, lighter fuels) and cleaning fluids can cause death through suffocation or heart failure.

Long-term health effects

Tiredness, poor performance at school and in sports. Possible lasting damage to body (liver, kidney, brain) but this is rare.

Law

Not controlled, but illegal to sell to known or suspected solvent misusers.

Tobacco

Nicotine is the drug effect of tobacco, a mild stimulant, found naturally in tobacco leaves. Cigarette smoke consists of droplets of tar, nicotine, carbon monoxide, and other gases.

Short-term effects

Nicotine has a complex effect on brain activity. Immediacy of impact is thought to contribute to the attraction of smoking, while the rapid decline permits frequent use. Smoking is linked with the alleviation of stress and anxiety and with maintaining performance in the face of fatigue or monotony.

LONG-TERM EFFECTS

The more one smokes, the more likely one is to suffer from heart and lung diseases, blood problems, and oral illnesses. Lung cancer is related to the number of cigarettes smoked per day, the number of years smoking, and the earliness of the age at which one started. Women smoking beyond the first months of pregnancy tend to give birth to smaller and less mature babies, giving rise to difficulties after birth. Oral contraception coupled with smoking causes an increase in heart or circulatory system diseases.

LAW

Prohibition of the sale of any tobacco products to children under 16. Strengthened by the Children and Young Persons (Protection from Tobacco) Act 1991.

SLANG

Smoke, ciggy, fag.

Appendix 2: Contacts

ADFAM National runs the national telephone helpline for families and friends of drug users. Waterbridge House, 32–36 Loman Street, London, SE1 0EE. Tel: 0171 928 8900.

Alcohol Concern provides a range of services relating to alcohol misuse including a library, publications, and information packs. Waterbridge House, 32–36 Loman Street, London SE1 0EE. Tel: 0171 928 7377.

DRINKLine – the national alcohol telephone helpline. Tel: 0345 320202.

Drug Prevention Teams – these Home Office-run teams work in local areas using a variety of drug prevention methods. Contact the Central Drugs Prevention Unit on 0171 217 8631 for details of your local team.

ISDD (Institute for the Study of Drug Dependence) provides a national drugs information service, library, research, and publications function on all aspects of drug misuse. Waterbridge House, 32–36 Loman Street, London, SE1 0EE. Tel: 0171 928 1211. E-mail: services@isdd.co.uk Website address: http://www.isdd.co.uk.

National Children's Bureau produces a listing of residential projects for young people with details of which will take solvent and drug users – 8 Wakely Street, London, EC1V 7QE. Tel: 0171 843 6038.

National Drugs Helpline is a free, confidential, 24-hour helpline service. Tel: 0800 77 66 00.

Network VSA is a national grouping of agencies involved in Volatile Substance Abuse issues. 53 James Street, Blackburn BB1 6BE. Tel: 01254 677 493.

Release gives information and advice on social and legal aspects of drugs. 388 Old Street, London EC1V 9LP. Tel: 0171 603 8654.

SCODA (Standing Conference on Drug Abuse) has a young people and drugs good practice unit and provides information on drug services in your area. Waterbridge House, 32–36 Loman Street, London, SE1 0EE. Tel: 0171 928 9500.

TACADE provides drug education training plus materials and publications on drug education and prevention. Tel: 0161 745 8925

Appendix 3: References

Baker, O (1997) *Drug Misuse in Britain* 1996 London, ISDD.

Balding, J (1996) *Young People in 1995 Health Education Unit*, University of Exeter.

Balding, J (1996) *Young People and Illegal Drugs in 1996 Health Education Unit*, University of Exeter.

Barrison, IG et al (1985) Adverse effects of alcohol in pregnancy *British Journal of Addiction* 80, pp11-22.

Bolton, P (1987) Drugs of Abuse. In Hawkins, D Ed. *Drugs and Pregnancy: human teratogenesis and related problems*. Edinburgh: Churchill Livingstone, p189.

Carey, P (1995) HIV, pregnancy and the drug user in Siney, C *The Pregnant Drug Addict* Midwives Press pp42-50.

Central Drug Co-ordination Unit (1995) *Tackling Drugs Together – a strategy for England*. HMSO.

Connaughton, J F et al (1997) Management of the pregnant opiate addict: success with a comprehensive approach *American Journal of Obstetrics and Gynaecology* 129 (678) pp7-8.

Department of Health (1995) *Sensible Drinking. The report of an inter-departmental working group*. HMSO.

Department of Health (1992) *Guidance for Local Authorities. Children and HIV* London.

Department of Health (1991) *Working Together: A guide to arrangements for inter-agency cooperation for the protection of children from abuse*. HMSO.

Fried, P (1986) Marijuana and human pregnancy in Chasnoff, IJ (ed) *Drug use in pregnancy: mother and child* pp64-74.

Goodwin, TM (1988) Toluene abuse and renal tubular acidosis in pregnancy *Journal of Obstetrics and Gynaecology* 71 (5) pp715-718.

Graham, K et al. (1989) Pregnancy outcome following first trimester exposure to cocaine in social users in Toronto *Veterinary and Human Toxicology* 31 (2) pp143-148.

Hanson, J et al (1978) The effects of moderate alcohol consumption during pregnancy on fetal growth and morphogenesis. *Journal of Pediatrics* pp457-460.

Health Advisory Service (1996) *Children and Young People: the substance of young need* HMSO.

Health Education Authority (1996) *Drug realities: national drugs campaign survey* HEA.

Hepburn, M (1996) Drug use in pregnancy *Druglink* 11(4) p13.

Hutchings D E (1993) The puzzle of cocaine's effects following maternal use during pregnancy *Neurotoxicology and Teratology* 15 pp281-286.

Ives, R (1995) *Problems with Solutions* London, ISDD.

Koren, G et al (1989) Bias against the null hypothesis: the reproductive hazards of cocaine *Lancet* 2(8677) pp1440-1442.

Leitner M et al (1993) *Drug usage and drugs prevention: the views and habits of the general public* Home Office.

Local Government Drugs Forum & SCODA (1997) *Drug using parents – policy guidelines for inter-agency working.* LGA.

Mounteney, J & Baker, O (1996) *DrugsCare* London, ISDD.

National Foster Care Association (1991) *Young People and Drugs* London.

National Local Authority Forum on Drugs (1989) *Drug Using Parents and their Children – issues for policy makers* London.

Northern Drug Services Child Care Group, Under 16s
Working Party (1991) *Drug Misuse and Caring for Children*
Grimsby Health Authority.

Parker, H et al (1995) *Drug Futures – changing patterns of
drug use amongst English youth* ISDD.

Peiris, G L (1987) Gillick v West Norfolk Wisbech AHA
Criminal Law Practice 40 pp93-112.

Perry, L (1982) *Women and drug use: an unfeminine
dependency* London ISDD.

Ramsey, M & Percy, A (1996) *Drug misuse declared: results
of the 1994 British Crime Survey* Home Office.

Rosett, H, Ouellette, E et al (1979) The effects of heavy
drinking during pregnancy *American Journal of Obstetrics
and Gynecology*, 51.

Royal College of Obstetricians and Gynaecologists (1996)
Alcohol Consumption in Pregnancy, RCOG Guideline.

Scottish Ministerial Drugs Task Force (1994) *Drugs in
Scotland: meeting the challenge*. HMSO.

Standing Conference On Drug Abuse (1996) *Through the
eye of a needle* London.

Standing Conference On Drug Abuse (1997) *New Options:
changing residential and social care for drug users*. London.

Tameside Social Services (1992) *Drug use by young people –
practice guidelines and procedures* Tameside Metropolitan
Borough.

Thornton et al (1990) Narcotic addiction: the expectant
mother and her baby *Irish Medical Journal* 83 (4) pp139-
142.

Welsh Office (1996) *Forward Together – a strategy to
combat drug and alcohol use in Wales* Welsh Office.

Wright, J et al (1983) Alcohol consumption, pregnancy and
low birth weight. *Lancet*, March pp663-665.